THIS U.S. CITIZEN

THIS
U.S.
CITIZEN

THOUGHTS AND CONCERNS OF A UNITED STATES CITIZEN

JAMES D. WERNECKE

□ □ □

For questions regarding publishing or copyright please write to:
This U.S. Citizen:
Attention Publishing
P.O. Box 3386
Cedar Park, Texas 78630-3386

ISBN: 1451509979
EAN-13: 9781451509977

Printed in the United States of America

10 9 8 7 6 5 4 3 2 1

First Edition

□ □ □

For Audrey, Lillian, & Samantha-
Conneene & Stephen-

Dedication:

This book is dedicated to those individual U.S. Citizens who throughout our history have stood up for liberty, freedom, and to protect the founding principles and ideals of the United States of America;

And to those who are about to...

This U.S. Citizen

CONTENTS

Introduction: Can We Keep It? 13

Chapter 1: Restating the Obvious 17

Chapter 2: The Disconnect 33

Chapter 3: Exceptional People 39

Chapter 4: ...will herald the end 53

Chapter 5: To Know One's Self 61

Chapter 6: The Right to Pursue 71

Chapter 7: Whatever evil they please ...79

Chapter 8: The Rightful Masters 87

Chapter 9: A Metamorphosis 97

Chapter 10: Trusted Leaders? 103

Chapter 11: Morally Treasonable 111

Chapter 12: The Natural Progress 119

Chapter 13: Enlighten the People 133

Chapter 14: Evils of Capitalism? 139

Chapter 15: The American Way 149

Chapter 16: Bias? 163

Chapter 17: Enemy of the U.S............... 169

Chapter 18: The Duty of the Citizen 177

A key to success is learning and using simple and proven ideas that work. One does not toss them aside due merely to their age or lack of novelty.

-James D. Wernecke

This U.S. Citizen

Introduction: Can We Keep It?

If at our country's beginning Benjamin Franklin expressed concern, should we not heed his warning today?

Many know this short bit of history but some may not. The deliberations of the Constitutional Convention of 1787 were held in strict secrecy. Anxious citizens gathered outside Independence Hall when the proceedings ended in order to learn what had been produced behind closed doors. A Mrs. Powel of Philadelphia asked Benjamin Franklin, "Well, Doctor, what have we got, a republic or a monarchy?" With no hesitation whatsoever, Franklin responded, "A republic, if you can keep it."

I recently thought about what could have been behind Benjamin Franklin's statement he made to Mrs. Powel as he left Independence Hall. The statement makes me wonder and speculate about the vast amount of time that was spent in the secret discussions as to the potential outcomes over time of the many different governing methods. They held the meetings in secret because they discussed openly the pros and cons of all known forms of government from monarchies, to democracies, to republics. Discussing the potential good aspects of living under a king or a military dictatorship would most likely not have come across well to the ears of the average person on the street so discussing in secret was probably the right thing to do at the time.

The founders had as an overriding theme in their discussion which was to create a government which would be the most difficult to alter and at the same time preserve the greatest amount freedom for the people. They were not only thinking of how to limit a group or any one individual from taking over the United States and controlling the people but also to subvert the shortcomings of human nature they knew could cause the potential faltering of a nation. I think it is these human nature shortcomings that threaten our republic today and we must realize it to take action and prevent what may be a perilous future for all of us and our children.

I believe this book may contain some of the concerns Benjamin Franklin may have been worried about when he uttered his statement regarding our new form of government.

Whenever I think about the direction of the United States, see what is going on in our country and hear some of the things people say, it brings me back to Franklin's statement and its importance. So I ask, if Benjamin Franklin was concerned the republic they had just created mere moments ago was fragile and had the potential to falter in the future, should we not today be just as concerned as he so vehemently was in 1787?

This has led me, an average United States Citizen to write down some of my thoughts and beliefs regarding where we stand today concerning the United States of America. I also state what this citizen thinks – *we the people* – need to do to protect our liberty and our freedom from those that think so little of it and even worse, do not even understand it.

Something just seems to be wrong. Is it just me or is American decaying in some strange and sinister way that will eventually affect us all. Is it already happening? This book is not about bashing America but is merely my observations, conclusions and some possible solutions to keep America the greatest of all countries and to maintain the freest society ever established.

I have been thinking a lot lately and wondering if these are merely my own worried thoughts or do others think like me as well? Are others worried about the direction of America, its people, and our way of life we have known for more than two hundred years. In the big picture America has only been around for a small tick of the clock and could disappear just as quickly I fear. The problem is, many cannot conceive the thought of America failing but reality and history says different. We can fail, and we will if we do not face reality of what works and what does not when it comes to governing a nation based on freedom of the individual.

I have a theory of which the outcome is unknown but not out of our control, not quite yet anyway. What I do fear is once a point is reached, there will be no way to return to what we have known to be successful in the past.

Is this book about politics? Yes, there are many aspects related directly to politics but I think this is a book more about human nature and what happens if human nature is left unchecked.

The Founding Fathers knew much about history and human nature and crafted the beginning of our nation to try to control the negative aspects of unchecked human nature and where it may lead. They were geniuses of their time and although not perfect, did very well at crafting this United States of America. They solved the problems they could and left the most difficult one, slavery, alone for the time being. I understand if they had tried to solve that problem then, it is doubtful they would have been able to give our nation its beginnings at all. The Civil War showed when slavery was indeed addressed; there were surely differences of opinion. Hundreds of thousands of Americans died because of those differences. The founders were proven right seven decades after the Constitutional Convention that tabling the slavery problem at that time was indeed the right thing to do.

Addressing the root problem at hand at the time showed a willingness to take risks and move forward instead of trying to solve all problems at once and wind up with nothing. They did what they could, the best they could and it lead to the founding of this nation. If you can solve 90% of the problems at hand, it makes sense to do so. More focus can then be applied to making the necessary improvements.

Chapter 1:   Restating the Obvious

> *We have now sank to a depth where the*
> *restatement of the obvious is the duty of intelligent men.*
>
> -George Orwell

First of all, let me say this book is a written account of how I see things in the United States today. It is not technical or statistical in my opinion but does reach some conclusions based on simple logic and reason about the unknown direction of our country and what may be in my opinion with high probability, influencing our nation's direction. I write as a concerned U.S. Citizen, nothing more. Is it a book, just random thoughts, a very long editorial column, or just a long rant from a citizen fed up with being told what is best for him by an over reaching government? I don't know. You decide and let me know.

This U.S. Citizen merely believes it is his duty to speak up. If my conclusions are correct then by not taking action to write these thoughts down to try to alter the current path, I am part of the problem. I believe my assessment is logical and reasonable and based on *common sense* - two words used often today but in my opinion, ***rarely utilized***. It seems to me it has taken about 200 years to reach where we are today. To understand the mentality of a large portion of those in America is important in order to make adjustments to preserve the greatness of the United States of America.

17

I write again not to criticize Americans but to help Americans face reality. We have flaws but those flaws do not outweigh the good done in the past and survives today because of the fact the United States of America exists.

I am writing for the most part in the first person from my point of view and based on my thoughts and concerns. I will from time to time refer to myself as "this U.S. Citizen" because it conveys how I now think more and more about myself, my role, and my duties as a citizen of our nation. I will from time to time use "we", as in We the People, because I want it conveyed these are the thoughts and concerns of individual U.S. Citizens and I do make an assumption I am not the only one with these thoughts about which I am writing. I believe this book speaks for many citizens that do not think they are being heard at this time in U.S. history. I write as a conversation and in the way I talk to my friends and family. It is meant to bring up points of discussion. The topics I am writing about are the issues concerning me and I hope many of you as well. It is merely my conversation from one U.S. Citizen to another.

I am sometimes non specific in some areas because what I am discussing is so obvious I do not believe examples are needed. If you are reading this book, I doubt if I have to point them out. I will probably say things here offensive to some people and some things will not apply to you. If it does not apply then do not worry about it, but if it does offend you, I just ask you to think specifically why you are offended and give me a logical rebuttal. If I am wrong, I will be the first to admit it.

Although not normally the way one writes a work or a project and since this is the first book I have ever written, my goal is to get my points across in a relatively straightforward way, just in case one of our representatives decides to read it. (Tongue in cheek)

Although I do cover my views of what I believe to be the major problems when it comes to our government I also touch on a few other subjects important to me. These are subjects I think more U.S. Citizens should be more comfortable discussing with others to increase the overall understanding of these issues instead of relying on government officials to tell us what we should be thinking. These areas stem from: government involvement in our lives, to basic economics, and includes the changing of our collective values and mindset from where it was at the beginnings of America to where we are today. Most of what I have to say is based on my perception of the current state of the U.S. regarding the role of government and the people, my views on war, etc.

I also have no expectation my thoughts and concerns or theories are of the overall sentiment in the country but as a U.S. Citizen I believe they are valid matters at least worthy of some consideration. My reason for writing is in the optimistic desire and expectation more people will get involved and stay engaged in the oversight of those in charge of our governance. It is our *duty;* for everything we enjoy relies on keeping government in its proper place, preventing its free reign over us, and to reduce and limit its meddling in our everyday lives. Such is my goal and why it is more important than ever that every U.S. Citizen get involved and informed regarding Politics and the dynamic influences it has on us all.

I am simply an ordinary citizen thinking out loud, or on paper, whatever you prefer. I am not much for adhering to a writing style. I hope it to be somewhat organized and I have the ability to get my points across. I have never had a real desire to be a writer and this will most likely be the only book I write but for some reason, I felt I must do it. I want to say the things I do not hear around me but seem to keep popping up in my mind. I want to ask questions of why and how the government of the United States of America is what it is now and what is likely to evolve from here. I have thought long and do not think I like its current direction. Some of my conclusions, many may disagree with and ignore as being too simplistic but this is part of the problem today. People have been convinced by intellectuals and politicians that life is very complex so they, the so called experts can come to the rescue and save us from ourselves. I disagree. Life is only as complicated as we make it and we could all do with a little perspective and get back to some very basic ideals to follow. We need a return to basic common sense and high moral standards with the expectation that people do make mistakes. Sometimes things will go wrong but to have the perseverance to continue to move forward and get better over time versus waiting around for something to happen or someone to do it for us.

Simple logic, those trying harder will succeed more. You will never hit a baseball if you do not swing at a pitch. Show me a person that does not try hard and often and I will show you a person waiting for something good to happen to them. Over time many of these people realize nothing is going to happen and they start looking for others to blame. Unfortunately, the blame is geared toward those that do try harder and more often. Animosity will emerge toward the wealth they have also accumulated by working harder than others. This is a flaw in the individual's ability to look at themselves for the source of improvement in their life and doing something about it versus hoping someone does it for them. Do we really live in a country where the early bird is no longer allowed to get the worm? If he gets up early to gather food but has to distribute it to those not bothering to rise with the sun, what is the purpose of getting up early? The initiative to be innovative and make difficult efforts disappears therefore any reason to not do as little as possible emerges as the norm. Is it a healthy society that fully depends on successful people for survival and yet denigrates and destroys their success at the same time? Is it too much to ask that *everyone earn* their keep?

Some may very well dismiss what I write as nothing more than a bunch of throwback ideals having little relevance today. This again is part of our problem. Discarding the basics in lieu of the new and seemingly fresh ideas without thinking through the potential unintended consequences is just a bad idea. There are some things that never lose their importance. To change for the sake of change alone is a game only those with the inability to think engage in. I would also venture to say those engaging in such an action should be avoided completely.

These issues are important because those in charge of our government need to know what we the people are thinking. They need to be forced to not only listen but to *hear* us. Our government's failure stems from the fact our representatives are not only out of touch with the people electing them, but also out of touch with their *duty* of holding public office. America is beginning I fear to lose the focus and the importance of the freedom of the individual or the "I" representing each one of us. The Founding Fathers knew freedom of the individual and his property was the key to a long term free society.

I am also writing because this U.S. Citizen is worried. I am worried and for me, this is unusual because normally I can detach myself personally from most negative details in my life. I usually deal with problems, deal with the outcomes either good or bad and move on. What I cannot ignore any longer is what is happening to my country. Why in the last few decades have we gone in such a direction?

Today it seems we live in a time where no one can make a judgment call about anything or anyone and if you do, you are looked at as close minded, short thinking, or just mean. Is this not itself a judgment made by the non-judgmental crowd? A bit silly to me but it is serious because it works its way into our everyday life. We cannot tell a co-worker to speed up what they are doing else you take the chance of them taking it as a personal attack or as being harassed. Decisions today must be made by a *consensus* together with everyone including those that know nothing about the issue at hand. Why is it today offensive to say some people are indeed just smarter about some things than others?

This consensus regarding everything mentality has a built in premise the thoughts and ideas of a single individual are not valuable compared to those of a group. I believe this is just wrong. If something is the right thing to do, it is the right thing to do no matter the idea came from a group or an individual person. Thinking of this sort just slows everything down. Everything we do has to be thought about several times to assure no one is offended. It is an impossible task because there will always be those who are offended by something. Political correctness is run amuck and is infecting our very spirit as Americans. We are more worried about sheltering the fragile feelings of some and willing to forgo or delay needed action because of it.

One example is the seeming growing trend of not keeping score in young kids' athletic events so no one has to be on the losing side. I also hear that trophies are sometimes given to all participants simply for showing up. This instills an expectation of getting a reward while doing nothing, very little, or even substandard work to earn the reward. How is this a lesson for real life in

America this U.S. Citizen asks? It is not. I believe it creates a mindset very young that will be slapped down hard with reality as they grow up. If kids are not prepared for failure, how will they recover when they do fail? What is it creating this trend in the way people are thinking today?

Speaking of being slapped down by reality; political correctness has now proven to be deadly. I am referring specifically to the terrorist attack on the soldiers of Fort Hood where thirteen people were murdered by a fanatic Muslim who displayed signal after signal he may be dangerous and yet nothing was done to prevent his killings due primarily to political correctness. This event really hit home because Fort Hood is only about an hour and a half drive from my home.

After the attack when I heard General Casey talk about the army and how diversity was its strength and how it would be worse if diversity became a casualty. I was disgusted. So, diversity is more important than the lives of his soldiers? When I heard him utter his statement, I knew we have now reached a tipping point where political correctness endangers our nation. Do you protect diversity by the purposeful act of ignoring sign after sign an Islamic extremist is in our very ranks? Is that how to protect diversity? By risking soldiers' lives? Political correctness is a poison infecting the fabric of our country. Innocent people serving their nation were brutally killed on their own soil because of it and I am sick of it.

Political correctness is anti free speech. Free speech means we have the right to say things that just might offend some people. If it did not offend anyone, why would it need to be protected by the Constitution in the first place? When you cannot even say something is wrong just does not look right because *we don't know the underlying circumstances* or what may have *contributed* to the event, we as a nation are dead, just like those Fort Hood soldiers. To Hell with what is causing it! You fix it now, you end it, you kill it, and you stop it. Then you worry about how it happened. By trying to ignore the Islamic influence here we are opening our chest to be stabbed through our nation's heart and turning our head so we do not see it coming. This is insanity. We can make no judgment about anything anymore because some think there is always a justification or underlying causes for anything anyone does.

Well I say BS and this is just wrong. Most of the time the writing is on the wall and you do not have to *jump* to conclusions to know what happened and how to fix it.

What is the remedy you may ask when it comes to correcting the dangers of political correctness in the lives of citizens, our work lives, and the safety of our nation and its people? One, we must have the courage to call people out that appear to be doing the wrong things. (Judgment alert) Two, we must be allowed to call those out who do not pull their weight in society. (Judgment alert, hurt feelings may be a result.) Three, Identify,

identify, identify the enemy and eliminate them, period. (Judgment alert) We must be allowed to make judgments based on current information and act on them to protect our lives and our freedoms.

> *Evil flourishes when good men do nothing.*
> -British statesman, Edmund Burke

America is different from the rest of the world because its system was based on the rights of each individual. Every individual person has rights of self interest and due process of law equal and even exceeding any group and is protected by the Constitution. When a group overrules the rights of an individual, this is mob rule.

It is time to stand up and be counted but more importantly to stay up and stay involved in safeguarding the United States by safeguarding its founding principles of liberty and freedom. It is our duty and our turn in history to offer our time and energy to protecting the gift passed to us. We must not let it slip back into the darkness due to natural tendencies of human nature and complacency.

To create and preserve great ideas is difficult and we must take on the challenge because we now have no other option. So although these ideas and statements I make are simple, solid, and easy to understand, we must remember that any good structure is built on such foundations and their importance must be revisited, and repeated, and often.

I do not believe myself to be an overly intelligent person but I simply believe I have reached a point where I can filter the unimportant distractions of our every day lives thereby clarifying my focus. This allows one when needed to return to basic principles of integrity, courage, accountability and truth. To this a quote from George Orwell comes to mind: "We have now sank to a depth where the restatement of the obvious is the duty of intelligent men." However intelligent I may or may not be, I believe am worthy of this duty and many other U.S. Citizens are as well.

Who am I to think I know what is happening? I'm no one special. I am from a small town in Texas with a population of about 1,000 people. I went to the same school from Kindergarten to graduation from high school. I am also a former U.S. Marine, but as Marines go, you never stop being a Marine your entire life. You just gain a little weight here and there. I served from 1991-1995 and saw no combat so I do not speak as a war veteran. My enlistment included ongoing training in an artillery unit, a peacetime overseas deployment, and participation in several humanitarian missions. These humanitarian missions included aiding victims of Hurricane Andrew in Florida to rescuing Cuban and Haitian people from the Caribbean Sea who were trying to escape their tyrannical, impoverished, unstable, and oppressive countries.

My time as a Marine though very short gave me perspective for my life, although I understand it better today than I did then simply due to age and maturity.

This helped me appreciate just how lucky I am to have been born a free citizen of the United States of America; the freest nation ever to exist. This small bit of travel and exposure to the rest of the world and to other people gave me the desire to achieve more, see more, do more. I am the first person in my family to earn a college degree which I completed after leaving the military. This was part of my mindset change I had in the military which was to not just wait for something good to happen to me but to start making it happen. After high school I wanted nothing to do with going to college because high school was boring to me and I figured college would be more of the same.

Waiting for things to happen instead of making them happen is what I did for a few years after high school. This lead not only to idleness of my body but worse, idleness of my mind. Finally I did come to the realization I was wasting my life and something needed to change. I needed to create new paths for myself. Going into the unknown would create paths that would begin to open new and before unseen opportunities and knowledge thereby creating even more opportunities. *This* is what America is about. Joining the military is what I chose. Not the Marines at first but a very persuasive and impressive Marine recruiter caught me leaving the Navy recruitment office one day and he had me. I did consider the other branches as well but I decided if I was going to join the service, I was going to choose the one I knew would be the most difficult. I was hungry for a challenge. In many ways it was difficult.

Culture shock was a big one but what I learned is just how adaptable I was to this sudden lifestyle change and how things are really not as bad or hard as we think they will be once we make the decision and go forward giving 100% honest and dedicated effort. One thing about being a Marine is that it teaches you new respect for getting a good night sleep and always having warm feet.

I had taken a step toward the unknown and out of my comfort zone which put me on a path that would expand my ability to think more critically, especially about myself. This one decision is what I think saved me from what would have been a very different life than I have now.

So what did I learn from this I think others should at least think about? Well, we have to pass on a belief that it is ok to fear the unknown but we cannot ignore it and we will have to venture into the unknown in order to grow. If we do not, we stagnate and die, not only as an individual but as a nation as well. This is the spirit of those who first came to America and founded our country. This spirit of adventure and the wanting of a better life is the basis of the values of those first settling America. These were not *American* ideals at the time but were the values and traits that made America great and created the atmosphere leading to the founding of the United States of America. This American spirit will strengthen and assure the United States of America and its ideals of exceptionalism will live another 200 years or more *if* we can simply get back to it and get the government out of *our* way.

We must force open the door of the unknown, each of us in our own lives as individuals but we must also maintain the freedoms with which we are born, endowed by our Creator, and protected by our Constitution to do so. This is where I think we are beginning to weaken. Our government is stagnating us, the people. You and I know when we depend on others or the government we have to play by their rules. Being responsible for ourselves and not on another or the government is the only way to preserve our individual freedom. Their rules are in place to benefit them and their bureaucracy, not you or me. The more of us who depend on the government for answers to our wants and needs, the more it grows. It is inevitable.

Government can only do at this point what we allow it to do but there is a point where our ability to limit our government will have been taken from us if we allow it. It has happened in every society. I say again, in every society to have ever existed in history. Human nature will be our downfall. It will happen unless we stop it. Not just by voting but by teaching and talking about the things I discuss in this book so people just do not show up to vote but know the reasons why they *must* vote. We must be an informed electorate in order to keep America great. It is my duty to try to make that happen. It is yours as well. Most importantly, we must help our kids understand how special the country they live in really is and pass on to them the responsibility and knowledge of how to preserve it.

I am a product of my environment, talents, and available resources. Most of what I believe and may repeat in this book very likely comes from the knowledge I have gained simply by reading as much as I can. If there is a book, paper, or article reaching my conclusion, I have not read it and would not have spent the time putting these thoughts into this book. It will require some very serious inner reflection. Having not read this particular theory or conclusion, I simply believe it may provoke some thought if not concern for the direction of the United States of America.

I will spend the remainder of the book speaking about what I think is hurting America but I think it will all tie back to one major theme we must confront in order to survive:

The mindset of Americans is being incrementally diluted from the mindset of the founding, original majority of people who had strong, personal internal drive to succeed, self reliance, and self-motivation; to a population where a majority may be without it. This is only made worse by a government which induces more of us to be dependent upon its benevolence.

This U.S. Citizen

Chapter 2: The Disconnect

My tipping point as to why I decided to write down my thoughts is that I really just needed an outlet for my frustration due to recent political events of 2009. I am referring specifically to the treatment of everyday, ordinary American citizens and how they were treated by their representatives and the media regarding the town hall meetings of the fall of 2009. I have reached the tipping point and firmly believe we are not being listened to by our representatives and senators. The only time they pay attention to us is at election time when we are bombarded by junk mail and endless phone calls. After elections I get the idea they feel it is their right to do whatever they want and not have to pay attention to us. They believe they have complete autonomy with nothing holding them from doing what they want regarding setting public policies and the drafting of new legislation. They truly believe winning an election gives them a mandate to do what *they* want from then on and pay no mind to the voters who put them there. To them, voters are nothing beyond the election and do not have to be considered until the next election.

This was blindly evident in the town hall meetings that took place in the fall of 2009. Many of our elected officials cancelled town halls to avoid angry constituents and although many did hold public meetings, it was apparent many elected officials held their constituents in utter contempt. This is their misunderstood meaning of being a representative. They are supposed to *represent* at least most of the ideals and views of their constituents and promote *those* ideals in the Congress and specifically not their own personal ideals. It is a vast disconnect and I believe the main reason why Congress at this point in history has such low approval numbers and why we the people need to remedy this. In my opinion, many of them think like this...

We do not elect them in the hope they make decisions we agree with!

It is supposed to be the other way around. They are supposed to do what *we* want them to do. Their job is to represent the people who elected them. Their job is to be *our* voice, the *peoples'* voice. If they are only beholden to their individual beliefs and make decisions based on that idea, how is that being a *representative?* Well I would venture to say, it is not. The setting up of the United States of America as a Representative Republic was done by the Founding Fathers for a reason. To elect someone to dictate their personal individual mandates over what they do in government as elected officials is not the reason. An elected representative gives up their own personal feelings and ideals to do what the people want him to do. Otherwise, what is the point? This is my definition of public service, or am I out of line here? This is why it is vastly important to only elect people we are sure are representing publicly and privately *our* ideals. If they cannot tell us directly and exactly what they believe, we cannot trust them enough to elect them

34

to represent us. Wishy-washy answers to questions can no longer be tolerated by a candidate or AN INCUMBANT.

I want to give an example of my experience at a town hall in the fall of 2009. I currently live in a republican district and my congressman is known as very conservative in his words and actions. I have voted for him and at the time of the town hall I felt good about him. I was hit with the realization during this town hall that once these reps go to Washington, something really does change them, and not for the better. A person in the audience asked the congressman what were his thoughts on term limits. The congressman's response struck me as the ultimate in arrogance. He basically said it is tough for new congressmen when they go to Washington. There is really no one to show them the ropes and it takes them a very long time for them to figure out how things work in Washington. He then said quote "we should let them keep their office at least long enough for them to vest their retirement." Again, we were told this by a very conservative Republican congressman from Texas. My jaw hit the ground when he said this and many of us in the crowd just looked around at each other in disbelief at what we had just heard.

From my perspective this is the same as telling me he thinks doing what it takes to get re-elected every two years is the priority for congressmen and when they reach their retirement vesting goals then they would start doing what is right for the people and the good of the United States of America.

Umm... NO! It does not work that way. This is when I knew even the most supposedly conservative person who goes to Washington can still be routed by human nature and focused on what is good for him instead of worrying about what he should be doing for the good of those who elected him to his office and for our country as a whole.

The fun time is over for us, for a while anyway. It is time we as individual U.S. Citizens started paying attention again and controlling our government instead of it continuing to increase control over us. We must get more involved, talk about government, and especially the Constitution, what it means and why the preservation of its ideals is important for our future. We cannot go years or even months any longer without keeping tabs on our officials. Our representatives and senators are imperfect human beings and we must choose them more carefully from now on and commit ourselves to their oversight. If we do not, human nature will eventually lead them back to where they are today, impotent and ineffective at doing Americans' business.

The fun time must be over for them as well. We must keep our representatives and senators more uncomfortable in their positions else they will take advantage of our lack of oversight. This I am afraid is where the problem lies and the solution lies with you and I. You and I need to constantly monitor our reps and if they do not do what we want, we must find new ones and get them elected as soon as possible. We must find ordinary citizens who will go into government with the expectation it may not be a permanent position. It will be hard because one has to be somewhat wealthy and connected to even run a campaign and what ordinary citizen can afford such an endeavor? So we are somewhat saddled with rich people but this is fine with me just as long as they support policies providing opportunities that help the rest of us live successful and rewarding lives for the most part. Is this really too much to ask from our reps and senators?

Somewhere along the line, our reps have got the idea their job was to go to Washington not to represent their constituents, but be beggars for them and to bring home the bacon or money to their districts or states. They do this by earmarking or creating legislation which would be unlikely to get passed on its own but is then attached to bills originally created for other major purposes like budget bills. Bills such as these are very likely to pass because budget bills keep the government or military running and what rep would vote against that?

When the bill passes, so does the earmark and then here comes the money to the district of the rep or senator who included it all courtesy of and taken from the tax paying citizens of the United States *without* their consent. This is a pretty easy way to try to justify your job come election time right? Sounds more like outright vote buying to me. This tactic is also used to pass bills which are short congressional votes and by what this U.S. Citizen believes to be outright bribery of reps and senators by adding things to bills that benefit them and their district in order to get their vote in the House or the

Senate. If I as a U.S. Citizen tried to pay a rep to vote for something I could go to jail, however when those in congress do it with the taxpayer money, it is called the legislative process. Even if the money went to my district I would still call it corruption. I hope you would as well.

Chapter 3:   Exceptional People

I have become a student of human nature, the understanding of people's personalities, and their character. I have been awakened in the past five years by maturity, age, reading, and observing people. Reading has made me aware, aware of history and of the people who shaped it. In books I have read there is the continuous question of what shapes people. Is it nature or nurture? Are people shaped by what they are born with i.e. the natural talent they possess? I think some people are born with natural talent for music, art, as well as math or science for example and this usually leads them into their lifetime profession or at least it should in my opinion. This is not to say anyone without a natural talent for these things cannot learn them, not at all but they may never be *great* at them. *-I heard or read that from someone but I cannot remember who so I am privileged to repeat their words, whomever they belong to.-*

On the other hand many believe people are products of their environment and its influences on them as they grow and mature. I really believe all people are talented at something and a lifetime of experiences is what leads to who we are as a person. It is of my opinion that natural talent plays a larger role but a person's environment forces the direction of what people do with their talent. In some cases the stars seem to align and it is easy to succeed. Having natural talents as well as being born into a family with connections or resources to aid those greases the wheels so to speak. This takes place when the talents are obvious and one understands their abilities and can benefit from the environment they were born into. However a person born into a situation with vast resources but with little or no recognizable talent may be doomed to the life of the spoiled rich kid. Unfortunately for many of us, I think these are the people who gravitate toward politics and to all of our detriment in their effort to prove themselves to someone, anyone, usually themselves. To prove themselves worthy they must meddle in other people's lives because they truly believe they know better.

One of my talents I believe I possess - *and I am sure I am offending someone when I say I think I have a talent* – is that I believe I can easily figure out people's motives and what people are thinking by the actions they take, things they say and how they say them. It is not rocket science and maybe it is not a talent at all but I also fairly quickly determine personality types of new people I meet. Just a quick note, when you match other people's personality type it makes getting along with them much easier. I would call myself a student of people. This probably sounds boring to most but this is something I think about quite often.

I want and like to know what drives people to do what they do and why this is interesting in the context of this book is that I wonder what were people thinking when they came to America so long ago? What type of people were they? What were they like? What personalities may have dominated the people who came to America? What talents did they possess? Think about the mindset of those who came to America hundreds of years ago and even today. Words which come to mind to describe these people include: motivated, head-strong, determined, not easily distracted, goal-oriented, focused, serious, risk taker, and optimistic. These are positive character traits in my book.

What drove these people to make such risky decisions such as crossing oceans to reach an unknown and potentially dangerous new world? Is this kind of *drive* something everyone possesses? I am willing to step out on a limb here and say no, I do not believe so. If there is one thing I have learned in my short thirty-nine years and really only over the past five is that people act and think very differently. There are many different types of people with very different personality traits such as: *outgoing, loud, quiet, introverted, friendly, coarse, smart, not so smart, happy, sad, helpful to others, uncaring of others, distant, depressed, anxious, strong-willed, stubborn, talkative, of very few words, analytical, driven, hard-nosed, flighty, focused, unfocused, highly dependent on others, independent minded, self-reliant, good listeners, bad listeners, dependable, undependable, trustworthy, shallow, selfish, unselfish, risk takers, risk averse, talkers, do-ers, direct, decisive, indecisive, humble, snobby, rude, open, expressive, dedicated, etc.*

I believe people and minds which think alike will automatically come together mainly because they are interested in the same things. It's the old *birds of a feather flock together* adage. Although there is the other

41

adage which says opposites attract but I think this to be the exception and not the rule. For example I am a very direct, a person of few words in conversation who does not beat around the bush. I absolutely abhor speaking with someone who does not ever get to a point and many times do not even have one. I find those people annoying and I bet they find me just as annoying at my lack of interest in participating in their chit chat sessions.

Now my point; does it not make sense the majority of those who came to and founded America and the United States were people cut from the same cloth and most likely had traits such as: *risk taking, outgoing, strong-willed, analytical, driven, focused, independent, decisive, dedicated, serious, and most importantly self-reliant?* These people were in fact, *do-ers.* They were essentially people who were not afraid to make decisions, were able to deal with adversity, and got things done. Those who were not do-ers and did not possess these traits were left behind in the old world.

The people who came to America had talent but had little or no resources in order to use their talents. They came here because they were *driven* by a want for a better life for themselves and their families. They were willing to take chances and risk everything including what little money or possessions they owned, and their very lives as well. They came to escape tyranny, to have religious freedom, and to seek a life where they were their own decision maker. People who came were decision makers who took action and got things done. They did not wait for someone else to decide for them.

They were not part of the *wait and see* crowd or what some call *fence sitters.* Those people waited for others to act and to see the outcomes before they did anything. These fence sitters were left behind by those willing to go into the unknown. People came to America because they were curious and had the mentality of those who were the original explorers. They were people who believed there must be a better life than the one they were currently living and *were willing* to seek it out.

I would venture to call those first people who came to America; exceptional, ergo *American Exceptionalism.* These people are high achievers and are those who go the extra mile, not satisfied with something which may be *good enough*, but that strive for the highest possibility, sometimes failing along the way. The unfortunate fallout that stems from the success of America is eventually those without exceptional talents begin to come as well to benefit from what is here. They want the benefit but they still do not possess the drive to earn it, thus dependency begins to grow and exceptionalism overall, begins to decay.

Those who came, the majority were not privileged people but an over-abundance of exceptional and driven people *was* the majority. If they were privileged, they likely stayed where they were because they were comfortable. Opportunities in America pulled a great amount of the cream of the crop (from an internal personal drive standpoint) away from Europe and its socialist and tyrannical ways.

Unknown opportunities pulled these people away from the rest of the world and these were the people who passed on the values and traits which contributed to making America exceptional. Here is a critical opinion of mine: I do believe exceptional and talented people and those without such talents are *not always* born of the same or vice versa and no one can control whether their offspring will be talented or have the internal drive to improve themselves to succeed. Especially having grown up in a free American society and somewhat comfortable compared to where their ancestors came from. These are now *American born fence sitters* who may now be creating a new majority of stagnant thinking and basically comfortable people.

They are comfortable in that they are not driven to make a better life for themselves. Especially not driven or motivated enough to cross oceans to an unknown and unpredictable life. It seems so many people are satisfied with their life today as long as they have the latest cell phone and the television comes on when they hit the remote. Is this not equivalent to the fence sitters of three or four hundred years ago who were satisfied as long as they had a loaf of bread and no one shooting at them?

America was a melting pot, but a melting pot of people who were the most driven and *unsatisfied* people of Europe and the rest of the world. Never has there been such a large aggregate of like minded, success driven people as those who first came to America. Finally free from oversight and decisions of others on their very lives. They wanted to be free to act, free to move on and leave those behind who could not make decisions or slowed them down. These people had a *take no prisoners* attitude and I think there is nothing wrong with that. They did not want to work for another or slave for another person's gain but were people who believed one must pull their own weight and had no use for those who would not.

These were people with a need to get more out of life, who had talent and drive and little resources but were willing to jump at the opportunity to immediately leave everything behind and leap into the unknown. *This is the American Spirit.* The ability to make a decision and go for it while willing to risk failure at the same time. They were tired of being told what to do by others they did not know or care about. I firmly believe America was built by those with the talent and drive to succeed but had little resources or connections to aid them. Freedom is what allowed them to succeed, Freedom. The incremental erosion of this freedom is what is now hurting this country.

These people who came to America across an ocean were now isolated from people who did not think like them, the *fence sitters.* Do you think this would lead to a new society of people basically mirroring where they came from? Doubtful. What would be the likely outcome of an isolated group like this? What type of country or nation could it lead to? What would it look like in the future and most important, *could it last*? It lead to the founding of the United States of America. Whether it could last is yet to be known.

What would happen if this original, temporarily isolated society of high achievement began to be diluted from within, decreasing the number of do-ers compared to fence sitters over time? If high-achievement and exceptionalism is no longer the mindset of the majority of Americans, what kind of leaders will we put in charge of our governance? What kind of society will result from this?

There are and will always be those people who will always find things wrong with anything. These people are the fence sitters of today. Those not willing to take a chance but will damn sure let you know how they think you did wrong after the fact. These are the people to stay away from. They are afraid to act and will criticize you because you make them look bad. They look bad because if you are found to have made the right decision, it shows their lack of courage and puts it on display for all to see. They simply cannot handle it. They will find faults no matter how right you were. If you are wrong they will let you know they told you so, determined to make you understand how they were right all along not to act. The mentality of these types of people is detrimental to America and is the same mentality as those comfortable enough not to take the journey to the new world. Our ancestors were smart enough to leave them behind hundreds of years ago. We must leave them behind in our everyday lives today for they will do nothing but hinder us and our nation.

The unwillingness to take the available information and move forward versus doing nothing to avoid potential consequences and sometimes even scorn from others is stagnating to us. Why have so many of us lost the American spirit of adventure to see what happens when we take that difficult next step, to put ourselves out there, and to take a chance? Where would we be now if the Founding Fathers had decided since solving the slavery problem at that time was impossible and they should not bother with creating a new nation based on freedom? Yes, a new nation based on life, liberty, and the pursuit of happiness, but where certain people were excluded is contradicting to me of course but they knew there had to be a starting point. They were willing to try a grand experiment. I am glad I am here now enjoying what America has become since the experiment began but am now very worried about the next step in our nation's future.

The founding of America was the first time in history where a majority of people who were high achievers, self-motivated, had high moral standards, and were self-reliant people had come together in very large numbers. This is part of the American *culture* of the United States of America. These unusually large numbers are now I fear, reverting back to the average of the rest of the world. This average has always been and is the norm in most other countries. We are at a crossroads looking at a situation which has never really occurred to this extent. America has been a high achieving culture and I think this culture is fading due to the natural progression of time. What we do at this crossroads is critical and I do not think there is a path

47

back unless some drastic changes are made. Can you imagine a country as great as ours going from what we are today; in the upper part of productivity and success scale and standard of living to merely a country that is average? I don't know about you but I like being freer than every other country in the world. I like living in a country with a very high standard of living with numerous opportunities to succeed. I like my rights being protected by a strong Constitution and Bill of Rights. My fear however is if we do not face the fact this relatively simple argument might be part of the reason for decline in overall drive and determination, we could be doomed.

No society has gone from such a high – productivity wise - to where we may be heading fairly shortly. What does it look like? I hate to imagine but I know it will not be what we know as freedom today. We may still be a free society, but I fear it will be a society where we are free to do as we are told. Free to live where you are told, free to earn how much is decided you *need.* Wait, is pay not being now dictated, I mean *regulated* by government officials now in certain types of businesses? I think we do have a *pay czar* do we not? Isn't this what the administration calls the person who makes sure pay is not too excessive for some CEOs? I have a question; excessive compared to whom? Why do they get to decide what is excessive? What is their definition of excessive based on? If this can be done to the big boys on Wall Street, don't you believe they would not think

48

twice about doing it to us if and when they deem it necessary for the sake of *our nation's interest*?

One more thing regarding and why I hate our government using the word czar; does anyone know where this word comes from? It comes from Julius Caesar, Caesar, and Czars from Czarist Russia. These were *rulers* from our world's past and yet it is used by our government as a cute nickname for an unelected government official.

So my conclusion here would be that some people are inherently more driven than others. Some are just willing to do more to get what they want and their personality traits and natural abilities influence their actions. I guess it is unfortunate everyone is not born with this kind of drive but is it anymore surprising everyone is not born with the ability to throw a one hundred mph fastball or compose music like Mozart? Why is it if you are a highly talented athlete or movie star and get paid millions of dollars, the pay czar does not show up on your doorstep but if you run a business you are held to different standards, government forced obligations, and where fairness and equality of pay suddenly apply? It is not my fault I cannot act or do not have a cannon for an arm so where is my cut of *those* people's earnings to make it fair to me? If it is a stupid argument looking at it one way, why is it not just as stupid from the opposite view? When government inhibits business through *over* regulation it kills jobs; jobs which would have existed as opportunities for citizens to earn a living, take care and raise a family.

This is a travesty of our freedom created solely by governments so called infinite wisdom.

It turns out the people born with the natural talent and abilities to succeed and manage a business are the ones who make most of the money. I think this to be the same as the most talented athlete or the highest grossing movie star getting paid the most to do what they do best. What is the difference here? People are born with very different personalities, strengths, talents, and abilities. Some people are just better at some things than others. I believe America started with a population of do-ers and now, this is fading. If you are a do-er, you know it and you are most likely confident with your abilities to make things happen. You will not need me or anyone else to tell you so. If you are not a do-er but a fence sitter, it doesn't really matter because unfortunately, I doubt you are reading this book.

Some might think my conclusions are a negative against America or some Americans. I see it as a problem which needs to be addressed because if it is not, the potential damage which could ensue on our country would be a tragedy. Many may be dismissive of my conclusions because I do not really have scientific or measurable data on which to base my conclusions but how would measuring this ever be possible? One simply must be able to see the big picture of what is happening today by applying simple reasoning to draw conclusions and although you may not believe or agree with me, I do not think you could say I have not made a logical argument.

Is what I assert as the reason behind the slow decay of our society really so far fetched? I think some may outright deny it because what it does is make each person take a serious look at themselves and decide if they are a do-er, and therefore more inclined to be successful in life or not, or go on with their life being a fence sitter.

Successful people make things happen. Unsuccessful people wait for things to happen. Risk takers and pioneers get the reward but also face initial failures which come with dealing with the unknown. These failures are necessary to find solutions to problems and should not be looked down upon and second guessed by those not willing to take the risk. It does not take a genius to Monday morning quarterback. The difference in *real* successful people and those who never quite make it is the latter stop when they fail or hit opposition. The truly successful march through adversity and keep going using the experience gained from failure to better themselves and their strategy. When you stop at adversity you have *convinced yourself* you have reached your limit and it is not useful to try again. Exceptionally successful people never accept such a premise!

This U.S. Citizen

Chapter 4: ...will herald the end

The reversion in America to the global average of the number of do-ers means the growing number of fence sitters have the potential to create serious problems because they will undermine the ideals on which this country was founded. It is of my opinion on average there are less highly productive or highly motivated people in the world than there are people who merely go along to get along. The latter being those who do just enough to get by. My proof lies in the fact America comprises only a small percentage of the world population but in its short life has produced more than any other nation in history.

America cannot continue to flourish if it is populated by fewer do-ers than fence sitters. It is a fact the do-ers earn a larger portion of the money and own a larger portion of all the assets than the fence sitters. This is due primarily to their higher motivation, drive, and desire to be successful and self-sufficient. Because the do-ers earn more of the money in America, they pay the much larger portion of the taxes than do the fence sitters. The problem which is occurring now is we are reverting to the average regarding the do-ers versus the fence sitter *mindset*, possibly damaging the very freedom and in that, the *attraction* of the United States.

When the fence sitters outnumber the do-ers it means we have reached a point where the fence sitters will control more votes than the do-ers. Because of our freedom and our so called participatory government, those now with the least or nothing to lose by increased government control have the power to take more from the do-ers of America. A fence sitter will always vote in a fashion giving them more without the concern of where their additional benefits are derived, as long as they get them. The do-ers have little or no recourse and more and more of what they earn will be taken due to this reversion to the average. Eventually, even the do-ers will see no use in being productive because any gain in life they make can and will be taken from them by a fence sitter majority vote through increased taxation.

> *When the people find they can vote themselves money, that will herald the end of the republic.*
> -Benjamin Franklin

If we get to a point where less than 50% of Americans are *drivers and are self-reliant*, it will closely equal a point where more than 50% of the population pays very little or no taxes at all. When those who pay very little or no taxes outnumber us, the country is doomed. They will always vote for policies giving them more and which cost them nothing. Little do they realize the only way to really know freedom is to become self reliant. Having never reached such a point, there is nothing for them to compare and they will unfortunately feel little remorse as they continue to vote away their liberty through empowering the government by supporting policies which create greater dependency.

This is the most important reason why we must now take an active role in controlling and leading our government instead of it forcing us in its inevitable desired direction. We have the power but we must have the commitment to stay engaged in our government. We can and will succeed because we are the drivers and the do-ers in America. We have the facts on our side and we must use facts to stop this overbearing government from running our lives *for our own good*. We have to keep going, learning from our mistakes while confronting bad policies and bad politicians when they are discovered. We must harness and focus our drive as U.S. Citizens to prevent the government from taking our freedom and our property. We must actively prevent the spreading and redistribution of our property to those who do not earn it and do not have the drive necessary to be a successful citizen. The critical time is now and we no longer have the luxury of sitting back and hoping someone else figures out how to solve our problems. *We are the solution*. The key is our representatives cannot be left alone any longer to work for the interest of preserving the ideals put forward in our founding documents. Human nature has taken them over, all of them and now we must be the overseers of our own destinies. The Founding Fathers set up our government to prevent human nature in a few from destroying the system but they could not create a way to protect us if a majority of our officials are corrupt. Corrupt meaning their acting in the interest of their personal goals of re-election and bi-partisanship instead of fulfilling their oath to protect and preserve the Constitution of the United States. There are simply less *American value driver personalities* in our government who are more than happy going along to get along. We must end this as soon as possible and return to instilling American values back in our families, children, friends, neighbors, and fellow citizens.

If we do not adopt this cause and make it an ongoing part of our everyday life, we will then be a nation of fence sitters, hoping and wishing things were different and wondering how all this came about. When a majority reaches a point where it can vote itself benefits from the public treasury, it will always choose to do so and with this soon follows a fundamental transformation and possibly the very collapse of our American society.

Only by electing officials with this understanding can we protect ourselves and our country by protecting our rights to earn money and keep the fruits of our labor. This problem is exacerbated by our legislators when they continue to focus their attention on increasing a voter base to try to guarantee their re-election. This focus means they are intent on actions such as creating more programs and entitlements for fence sitters through continuously increasing government spending. This increase in spending will demand more taxes from the do-ers to placate to the fence sitters for votes. This pandering gives no concern as to what the do-ers could do with their money or what positive impact it could have had on the economy due to the free market, had they been allowed to keep it. But then again, this is money which would have been spent in the interest of the do-er who earned it versus the potential votes it could buy for the legislator who took it for the *greater good*. Obviously our legislators believe they know what is best for us, the ultimate in arrogance.

Where is the focus on prosperity, economic growth, or creating opportunities for more job creation? You cannot focus on growing a voter base and re-elections while at the same time doing the right thing for all the people because you are catering to a specific segment of the people to the detriment others. So I ask this; how is the taking of one's freedom to pander to another in an effort to keep one's legislative position an accepted activity in American government? I do not believe this was the intention of the Founding Fathers and yet it is now our continuous cycle in American politics.

I think we are indeed approaching if not surpassed the point where the percentage of exceptional people on average in America has fallen due to natural occurrence over time. If this is happening and I am only saying it is a logical argument, what do we need to do to make up for it? Is this an expected possible result of a continuously growing government and we the people are becoming more reliant on it? Does it not make sense if the government does more, this will cause the people to do less and relinquish even more responsibility away from themselves? Will the next generation not even expect anything other than an issue taken over by the government to then be absolutely responsible for it from then on, never for the individual to have to worry about it again? If they, the next generation never had to deal with the issue, could they deal with it if the government returned the responsibility to the individual? Probably not, without problems to deal with. So would this not justify the government always remaining in control once it takes control of anything? Would the government use an excuse such as saying it would be too disruptive if the government did not control or continue to regulate an issue?

I think they would and do so. This proves the point to me our current government does not trust us to do the right thing if left with the freedom to do so. They believe we do not know what is good for us and they, being the experts they are, know better than we do about how to live our lives. This is what irritates me because I think this is really what they think of us, the ordinary U.S. citizens.

We have benefited from the traits of the original group of people who founded this country in more ways than most people can imagine. It is our responsibility to continue using the original mold the founders set up for us. Yes, adjustments are necessary but the *basic* American ideals must be preserved. The ideals inherent in the success of America are different from those throughout the history of mankind. These ideals are different because they are based on the individual's liberty and freedom. They are based on preserving the rights of each individual person first, above all other ideas. They are based on leaving people alone to let them do as they want as long as they do not injure others. America cannot survive if we allow this idea to be set aside in lieu of an idea based on forcing individuals to sacrifice for the greater good or for the benefit of others who will not do for themselves. If the Constitutionally protected rights of one individual person can be taken away by the government for the sake of another, then government can take away the rights of us all.

Preserving the ideals and traits behind the founding principles of America are difficult because it requires focused and constant effort. It requires constant *confrontation* of those who would toss these ideals aside. It requires confrontation of human nature and to fight against people's tendency to choose the easy path versus the uphill battle. Protecting freedom in the United States will always be a *permanent uphill battle* and we must come to grips with this as a fact! We have let it slide and now we must return to a vigilant and determined mindset. Whenever a new piece of legislation is discussed, the focus needs to go immediately to the question of its Constitutionality and scorn without end those people who do not take the question serious because it is *the most serious question* a U.S. citizen defending his freedom can ask. Bills which can damage the republic should be more scrutinized before becoming law instead of waiting for court cases to attempt to unravel a law's meaning in the midst of citizens drowning in the damage it is causing. We must intensify our focus on studying, brainstorming, and thinking about potential unintended consequences of actions taken today and the problems resulting from poorly drafted and completely incomprehensible legislation. If it cannot be explained by those writing it, how can it be understood by others either today or in the future? The understanding of our Constitution and our laws cannot be left to the subjective interpretation of any one person or one group else we live under the tyranny of continuous decree changes by *rulers* continuously striving to better their position at the expense of you and me.

Chapter 5: To Know One's Self

There are three things extremely hard: steel, a diamond, and to know one's self.
-Benjamin Franklin

The first generation of Americans was somewhat largely cut from the same cloth. They were determined, motivated, and even desperate for a chance at a better life. This desperation forces one to find a way to get things accomplished because there really was no option of going back from where they came. There was no plan B for them. America's success has today created too many fall back plans. Many people are now incapable of evaluating the factors necessary in decision making leading to many not making a decision at all, hence the increase in the fence sitter mentality. This I believe to be true for today's dithering people but this dithering is not a problem for those with the drive and motivation to move forward. America is great because it contains people who possess these positive characteristics, but let me return to those first few generations of people who came to America.

Again these first settlers were like minded people, talented people with little resources who left everything behind in aspiration of a new future for them and their families. There was no plan B or fall back plan for them and they knew it therefore they had to succeed or they died. Over time this mass of like minded people has slowly changed through the generations of the last two hundred years or so. Little by little as people had families and those people had families, we grew into a more dissimilar thinking group of Americans. The number of exceptionally minded, self-reliant, or high achieving people in relation to the number of average (*average meaning those without the traits of exceptional people*) has diminished. We as a people and a society are reverting back to the average of where our ancestors came from originally. I think this to be a natural occurrence and a very logical conclusion which explains much about what has influenced the direction of this country especially in the past one hundred years.

Regarding averages, no matter what one tries to do there will always be an average. Some people will be in the top fifty percent, while the other half will be in the bottom fifty percent. There is no way around it. In order to agree with my theory you also have to believe some people are inherently more driven to succeed than others. Everyone cannot be an above average achiever on an exceptional scale just as everyone cannot be below average. My conclusion is because at the beginnings of America we had a great deal more people come here from the top fifty percent of the high achiever mindset than from the bottom fifty percent, this was a very large factor which greatly contributed to America's success. Now that we are reverting to the mean where achievers are outnumbered by low or average achievers, America, as it has been known, *may* be in peril.

We are turning to a culture of jealousy; jealousy of the exceptional. Jealousy that someone else might have obtained something they cannot obtain with little thought as to how it was acquired. Jealousy of those who make more money, have a better car, or a better house will more and more tear at the fabric of American exceptionalism. The American dream will end when a person will not bother to better himself to earn or produce more because he will know if he does, he will not get to keep the fruits of his labor. Once this happens on a large scale, no one will produce anything of their own accord but will be forced to by government for the greater good.

This statement came from a comment posting from American Thinker.com: "*There are so many people in the United States that actually hate people that are successful and certainly those more successful than they are.*" I firmly believe this to be a true statement, unfortunately for us all. People with this mentality are dangerous to the American way and American ideals. Their focus seems to be to attack those who succeed instead of trying to learn from them how they became a success and use this knowledge to find success for themselves. Perhaps they may believe there is some magic piece of knowledge which will quickly and easily lead them to succeed however, when they find out success comes from working hard, being persistent, sacrificing leisure time, bettering your skills, and most important; having the ability to admit flaws in themselves, they refuse to accept it.

It is much easier to attack others than to face reality dealing with the fact the sole reason for their lack of success lies within themselves, in their attitude, and their limited outlook on life. They simply ignore the numerous opportunities available for them in the United States of America.

The opportunities here are limitless but there is one very simple strategy which can lead to success in my opinion and I would like to share it: *Most of the time you have to be willing to start at the bottom and work your way up over time.* There simply is no quick way to the top. You will have to do things you do not like doing for a while and I think this is what stops so many from succeeding today. Too many people today are just unwilling to do so. For some reason they think they are too good to do menial jobs or tasks. Instead, they want immediately the success others have and give little or no consideration of what it took or the time it took the other person to get there. When you start at the bottom, you learn the ropes regarding how things work, and because you are at the bottom, people know and understand your skills are limited for a while. There is no expectation you will do these jobs or tasks your entire life but these are starting points which will open new paths to a better future.

He that can have patience can have what he will.
-Benjamin Franklin

64

If you show you are willing to start low on the ladder and do what needs to be done *without excuse, complaint or attitude*, people will help you succeed. Successful people will tell you what you need to do but actually listening to the advice instead of simply waiting for your turn to give a rebuttal puts successful people off. Successful people value their time so if they get the idea you are not listening to them, they move on. Some will believe this just being mean and callous, but it is not. This is another reason they are successful. They do not waste time and resources that will not be productive and are able to make these decisions and judgments rather quickly based on their experience.

> *He that is good for making excuses is seldom*
> *good for anything else.*
> -Benjamin Franklin

To admit to one's self, let alone to others they are not pulling their own weight without using an excuse to bypass blame is a rare thing. It is more likely this happens much more today than it did by our country's founding people. It is a very rare event a person today can admit they screwed up and be honest with himself. People are too worried about what other people think about them, what others may say about them, or may ridicule them. It is almost as if some people are in a permanent teenager mode and nothing makes them grow up.

I myself, often question if I am making the hard choices or am I going with the flow, taking the easy path, or just following the herd so to speak. We all like to believe we are better than average at the things we do but the fact is, half of us are not. I hope at least this book will make people more aware of themselves and their direction in life. To know one has a purpose and is confident they are heading in the right direction makes all the difference in the world as to whether one is happy or not. Taking a hard look and having the ability to realize you could do better or do more for yourself is a key to happiness. Always having to look for an excuse is no way to live as an American. In fact, to be happy and successful in the United States of America, you cannot live a life of excuses. This is why some have such a hard time in the American business world. Feedback and reward is based on results, not intentions. If results do not eventually appear, actions are taken. More of us need to understand this fact. *This is how it is in America.* This is part of the culture of The United States.

It is easy to put things off for another day and necessary sometimes but we only fail if we do not step back and assess ourselves once in a while and are brutally honest about it. Brutal honesty may be what it takes to save our country from those who would usurp our freedoms for our own good. Being committed is hard; being proactive is hard; staying focused requires continuous and self-motivated effort. Yet these are the actions we must take to make up for those fence sitters who will not do what it takes. We must in order to remain free, protect our property and our earnings from politicians' good intentions, and to keep our country governed in the fashion created and envisioned by the Founding Fathers.

To succeed and to have a fruitful life in America requires knowledge. If you do not have this knowledge you must seek it out. Seek out successful people and ask them. They will help you but you must listen and be prepared and willing to accept criticism. The ability to listen and be self critical above many other traits will help you on your pursuit of happiness.

Some people think America is mean, a mean country with mean people and say Americans discriminate against other people. Well, I have to agree with this somewhat, America does discriminate, *it discriminates against the uninformed. It discriminates against the stupid, and so do I.* When I say stupid I refer directly to those who refuse to see reality and accept facts as they are, not how they want or assume them to be. I cannot remember but someone said: "Everyone in a free society is entitled to their own opinions but they are not entitled to their own facts." We must as U.S. Citizens teach the importance of political involvement and American ideals to our fellow Americans who may not understand them or have never been even introduced to them. It is our duty in order to preserve our republic.

It is difficult to encourage people to understand the realm of politics especially in a culture where vast numbers of us do not believe in starting at the bottom but seek instead seek *immediate gratification.* Well, politics is not an immediate gratification laced activity, except possibly when it comes to elections. It may take years and even decades for things to happen politically regarding policy issues. I truly believe the founders intended it to be this way. However, in our fast moving, cell phone, texting, immediate contact with everyone we know society, the slow motion of politics simply cannot compete. There are so many other fun activities to do. This is how we are taken advantage of by politicians. People do not pay attention and unknowingly have access to these very fun activities due exclusively to the freedom this country provides. Little do they know their lack of interest in politics and the protection of freedom will eventually destroy these activities forcing their attention on politics. At that point unfortunately, it is too late.

Permanent participation and education in politics is also difficult because it is hard for people to understand how they are affected *personally*. They have lack of interest because by the time they are affected, the news of the law is long gone and probably so are the people who made the laws. Most people do not participate because they get zero immediate gratification for their efforts. The election of Barack Obama is an exception. More immediate gratification seeking people than usual voted in 2008 because if he won, their payoff in participating in the election would be immediate and they had the opportunity to be part of what they believed to be an historic event. *Personal* payoff or gratification is usually never part of any election except to those who are majorly part of a campaign. I believe people voted for Obama in large part for the *quick emotional payoff.* I do not think contemplating his long term policy effects on the future of the United States had much of anything to do with it. If this was a concern, then what was the reasoning behind the lack of vetting of his public career before being elected to try to discover or even anticipate how his prior dealings might impact future policy decisions? It was never really considered seriously. People voted for him mainly for the immediate, emotional *delight.*

What unfortunately also plays into this is many people are disinterested in politics not only because of the personal distance or their belief politics does not affect them but they also are rarely given something important to vote *for.* So many people only go to the poles when they are frustrated and want to put a stop to a person or policies they feel are not going well; see President George W. Bush. In 2008, there were not only policies people wanted to put an end to but also something historic to vote for. People need something to vote for and freedom and American ideals should always be a clear choice on the ballot for them. If these things are on the ballot and part of a candidate's platform, people will show up and keep America great. If people only have to look forward to voting for the lesser of two evils, they will remain uninterested and America's ideals of freedom and liberty will falter *incrementally* over time.

When we only have the threat of losing a seat in office after the fact as the only action persuading an official to do what we want, we must seriously look more deeply at the character of candidates *before* an election and scrutinize them with brutal honesty and unending questioning. We must be more certain now than ever our elected officials will indeed take the actions after elections which are in line with their language from before the election. This all comes down to electing people of high moral character and integrity. *A politician who will say anything to get elected and tries to tell everyone what he thinks they want to hear is useless and dangerous to freedom and to our republic.*

Chapter 6: The Right to Pursue

The Constitution only gives people the right to pursue Happiness. You have to catch it yourself.
-Benjamin Franklin

It seems to me as though our government has morphed into an entity that actually encourages fence sitters to remain fence sitters. Government does this by keeping them just comfortable enough not to try to improve themselves for the better, which would turn them into the do-ers America desperately needs to remain strong. By not giving them too much however, they also prevent the fence sitter from really understanding what could be awaiting them should they get informed and contribute more to their own support by becoming self-reliant. *Government policies based on benevolence destroy the confidence people get from being self-reliant.* Government essentially subsidizes traits and values which are un-American thereby increasing un-American values in our people. When government subsidizes anything, you get more of what is subsidized. Good intentions do no matter.

Now that we are roughly one year into this new administration, I have concluded it is not focused on strengthening America or its citizens but is instead promoting and implementing policies which are weakening America, its values and its ideals. This focus appears to me that it is now payback time. This is payback against those who are more successful than others. What is so terrible is the tactics being used are going to spread misery to those of us who do make things happen in America so that we feel as helpless as those fence sitters that cannot find within themselves the will to self improve and create their own American dream. Because they cannot succeed themselves, they and their politicians think it is unfair for others to do so. It becomes their goal and they believe it will make them feel good to tear down *our* American dream. Essentially this feels like we are on a big playground where some are happy and others are jealous that others are happier than they are because of what they have or do not have. Please indulge me in this simple and possibly silly example because I think it makes a good point.

On this playground most people have playground balls to play with, and yes some are bigger and better than others but that is part of life in America. Someone will always have more than you such as a bigger house, nicer car and more money. To succeed and be happy and content in your life you must understand this because if not, you will live a miserable life wondering why your ball is not as nice or as big as others on the playground. But to return to my point about payback, it seems those now in control of our government are like jealous kids on the playground. Instead of teaching and learning to play and figure out how to obtain or create a better ball for themselves, they would rather use bullying force to take someone else's from them or pull out knife to cut the ball in half destroying its usefulness completely.

What does this accomplish? It robs the owner of his property in order to satisfy someone else's jealous wants. Now the owner of the ball is upset and angry at this loss and the person who took it has possession but still does not know how to make a ball for himself. If instead of taking the entire ball it is merely cut in half, this leaves two people with a half each. I don't know what kind of ball this was but it is now unusable for its original purpose which was to hold air, roll, and maybe bounce.

My point here is if this is the type of playground we all live on now, I will just want to take my ball, big or small and go home. I do not want to play this game anymore yet it is the very nature of government to prevent me from escaping its oppression. Government's goal is to continuously limit my avenues of freedom and box me into *their idea* of how I should live my life. This is nothing more than pure social engineering; it is the complete opposite of freedom and liberty in my opinion. I think our founders would be of the same opinion.

The real sad thing in this example is those without a ball on our playground did not realize -if they had just opened their eyes- they might have noticed there was a ball factory on the hill in the corner of the playground. All they had to do was read the instructions clearly posted on the factory wall, i.e. get informed. Then they would be able to enter, make or *catch* their own ball and return to the playground now confident in their ability to create the ball they desired instead of taking someone else's. If they had done so and now had the ball they desired I seriously doubt they would be happy if someone then came along and took theirs after they had worked so hard to *earn* and obtain it.

Although this is a very simplistic example, it makes the point but also may reveal something quite troubling. There are those on our playground now who refuse and absolutely ignore the existence of the *ball factory* on the hill. They refuse to see it themselves thereby eliminating its use as the best option for the playground residents to make new balls for themselves and be truly happy. They are blindly focused on punishing those with balls for the mere fact they have them. Those without balls are encouraged to despise those with them and are told it was not their fault they do not have a ball. This mentality justifies to some the taking from others and giving to those who do not have them. The problem which is not realized is when a ball is taken; the ball loses its bounce and will not roll very far or for very long. It makes them temporarily happy but when the ball 's attributes which make it useful deteriorate, it is useless and now the person who received the handout without earning it or learning how to make his own is without it once again. He still does not know how to create a new one. You see, a person's playground ball only keeps its bounce and usefulness if it is gained by learning where the ball factory is, reading the instructions, asking for help if needed, and making one for yourself and then sharing with others how you did it so they too can enjoy the fruits of living on this playground. Those who are self reliant ball creators pay the price of investing their time and effort into gaining entry into the factory on the hill. They paid their dues rather than wait for an opportunity to steal another's ball or have a *playground politician* create a program which entitles them to have a ball regardless of the reason behind their lack of ability to create their own. The problem lies in if the playground politician can get enough followers, he will take everyone's ball away and give them to whomever *he* deems worthy. At this point, any remaining ball owners will do what they can to survive. They will take their ball if they still have one and attempt to leave the playground if they can.

When America began, everyone pulled their own weight else they would starve. In our civilized society, this cannot be allowed to happen but *with that declaration*, so begins the cycle of one person doing or producing to not only sustain himself but others he does not even know at the *insistence* of a ruler or rulers. My question is: where does this lead? How much is enough? How much of one person's life is it okay to sacrifice in the name of the greater good of others, or fairness, or compassion? How in a free society does another person or entity get to decide how compassionate I am and determine how much of my labor is forfeit to meet *their* notion of compassion or benevolence for others?

In 1794, when Congress appropriated $15,000 for relief of French refugees who fled from insurrection in San Domingo to Baltimore and Philadelphia, James Madison stood on the floor of the House saying:

*I cannot undertake to lay my finger on the article of
the Constitution which granted a right to Congress of
expending, on objects of benevolence, the money of their
constituents.*

-James Madison
Father of the Constitution

So I ask, what percent of my income or what
reduction in my middle class lifestyle which I have
earned, must I give up? Under what evaluation criteria
does someone else determine the sacrifice of me -a
constituent, in the words of Madison- unto others? I
would like to know the numbers related to a definition of
when a person would be classified as a slave to their
society's goals. Is it fifty one percent of my income? Our
income *is indirectly our labor and a portion of our very
life spent doing that labor.* Those taking large portions
of our income are actually taking large portions of our
Life. This is an infringement of one of our most basic
rights as listed in the second paragraph of The
Declaration of Independence.

I think you as a reader should calculate how much
you pay to government mandates and taxes such as
income taxes, real estate taxes, sales taxes, government
fees, gasoline tax per gallon, federal regulatory licenses,
government fees and on and on and figure out what you
really get to keep for yourself and your family. Add it all
up. How much do you contribute to others' mandates?
Do that and ask yourself this question: Am I as free as

76

U.S. Citizens were fifty years ago, one hundred years ago, or two hundred years ago? If not, why?

This U.S. Citizen

Chapter 7:   Whatever evil they please

Government is authority and rule making over its people and our United States government today believes it has a blank check to create regulations, mandates and laws and where any action they take is Constitutional. I really do not think the question of Constitutionality ever really is considered and those in government merely do what they want and move forward as long as no one says much about it. When they get away with it, it reinforces their notion that we the people are uncaring, uninterested, or do not have the intelligence to understand what they do. More and more regulations simply mean it makes it more difficult for us to create and run our businesses and therefore, our lives. This applies to everything from a taco stand, to a car maker, to a home builder. It applies to everything. More oppressive regulations mean fewer opportunities for us, the people, while more control over our lives goes to those in government. Much of the blank check mentality in our government comes from a much skewed interpretation of certain parts of the Constitution such as the commerce clause and the general welfare clause.

It is my opinion and I assume many others, this is not the intended purpose of the commerce clause in the Constitution. In Article I, Section 8, Clause 3, the clause states the United States Congress shall have power "to regulate Commerce with foreign Nations, and among the several States, and with the Indian Tribes."

I believe it was intended, the government's job that is, when it comes to the commerce clause is; *to make commerce more regular.* In laymen's terms, make doing business easier by removing obstacles which hold people and businesses back, enforce contracts, punish those who cheat the system, and *streamline* processes. Does anyone else think our government is doing the exact opposite? Looking at if from this perspective is more in line with the overall intention of the clause. If what our government is doing today is not using *this* as their interpretation then I would like to know what they are using. Is it that human nature has taken over in these people and they have succumbed merely to *their* individual needs to enrich themselves or to meddle and tell us what to do for no other meaningful reason than that?

To insert a statement in the Constitution which basically allows those in our government to do whatever they want cannot conceivably be thought of as the intent of and in the spirit of the Constitution and the freedom it protects. The same applies to the aforementioned clause regarding providing for the general welfare.

They are not to do anything they please to provide for the general welfare.... Giving a distinct and independent power to do any act they please which may be good for the Union, would render all the preceding and subsequent enumerations of power completely useless. It would reduce the whole instrument to a single phrase, that of instituting a

Congress with power to do whatever would be for the good of the United States; and as they sole judges of the good or evil, it would be also a power to do whatever evil they please. "
- Thomas Jefferson

Surely neither of these clauses in the Constitution means it is justified to take close to half of what every U.S. citizen earns, or a large portion of what businesses earn to give it to someone else and say this is for the general welfare or in the interest of commerce? Am I the only person who feels as if their hard earned money is being squandered merely to assure re-election success?

Regarding this point of government interference, if the government taking control is the right way to solve the problems of Americans, how has it worked out so far? I would say not well. In 2009, I live in a United States where because the government takes so much of my income, an income which is not far from the average citizen, it would be impossible to have a single income home, where my wife could stay home and care for our twins due in February, 2010. I would like that to happen but it is unlikely. Some will say it is my own fault because we should reduce our lifestyle to do what is more important than money and I believe that but you can only reduce so much. I had not bought a new car since 2003 and would not have in 2008 if I had known company cutbacks and pay reductions were about to take place due to a failing economy. My home value is less than the average home value in the country and I will not apologize for wanting to live in a safe neighborhood with good schools in order to assure my twin girls will have a decent education and upbringing like I enjoyed. Is this too much to want out of life today as a U.S. Citizen? Is this selfishness? Really?

We must stop believing in the premise the government knows how to take care of those who cannot take care of themselves. They do not! When I say cannot take care of themselves, I specifically mean those who are incapable of providing for themselves. I speak of those disabled in ways making it impossible to function without assistance from others. Children cannot be expected to take care of themselves as well as the elderly who have reached an age where they can no longer rely on their body or mind to work in the way they need it to.

What I am not referring to are those who for some reason or another decide they will not work because they do not want to do certain jobs because they either do not like the line of work or feel like it is beneath them. These people believe they should not have to stoop to that level or start from the bottom. This is part of what is causing our problem and contributes to the over reliance on government assistance. *It is simply much easier to get on the government dole than to work.* It is that simple, is it not? What has created this sense of entitlement in so many people? Did the baby boomers spoil their kids so much by wanting and providing a better life for their kids the following generation(s) have become too spoiled to start at the bottom? The baby boomers did give their kids a better life, it is true but did they forget to pass down the reasoning behind it thus condemning future generations to expecting their just desserts without earning them? The desire for immediate gratification and the *comfortable* life they led with their parents creates a damaging state of mind. It makes people think they should immediately have everything their parents have at the beginning of *their working life* while giving no thought to the thirty to forty years of work and struggle it took their parents to make such an achievement. Their expectations as this point being their *starting point* in life will be a source of frustration for them when reality does not allow it except through excessive amounts of debt. These are debt levels we have now seen to be unsustainable and were a major cause of the financial meltdown of the past few years. Allowing people to have things they cannot afford at the insistence of government benevolence is detrimental to our economy as we now know.

Strong work ethics and high morals are not passed down like they were in the past. Many parents today are not *parenting* because they are too worried about being *friends* with their children. This parental failure of not passing down the morality of being able to live without dependence on or by taking from others is a rot at the core of any free society and will continue to be damaging to ours. Ethics and being of good character has decayed in just over two hundred years because passing down these ethical principles gets weaker and weaker as time goes by. I think of it as trying to make a print copy of a copy over and over for two hundred years. What would the final copy look like today? I would venture to say the final copy may have been degraded to a point where it may even be unreadable, *though not irreversible* if enough of us start actively pushing back against this tsunami of character degradation.

I will go another step forward and say I believe government confiscation of our earnings through excessive taxes for their programs has slowly diminished and may be destroying our abilities and to some, the desire to help others who cannot help themselves. If we the people had just half of what the government takes from us to provide for the so called *general welfare* we would have the resources to do more to help those in our local communities ourselves and without guidance from the government. I am not saying people do not do what they can now even with the taxes we pay but we should not be mandated by law with the expectation we would go to jail or fined if we do not. I know and have the faith people will help those in need and I think it would increase if we didn't have to support a government which does not listen to us.

One example comes to mind very easily. A family member younger than I and I am thirty nine years old was diagnosed with cancer and had no money, kids to feed, and faced leaving work for treatment. Very quickly a benefit was organized and in my part of Texas, that usually means a fish fry. Plates were sold and thousands of dollars were raised to help her get through the tough times ahead. It helped her and she got through it but the donors did not vow or were expected to take care of her forever. This is much different than government programs. Programs where a new expense is created, possibly with an automatic increase of six to ten percent per year to boot and would have been levied forever on the public.

Again this is just an example but unlike what you hear from politicians, people do not die starving or from lack of medical attention in this country. Even those who stand on street corners rely on normal people to help them out and many people do. If they did not they would not be on the corner the next day. People want to be charitable and many will. If there is a real need, people will fill it *if given the chance*. They want to and some people *need* to. This is not only good for those in need but is good for the soul of those who give. The government through excessive taxation and welfare programs takes this ability and opportunity to be charitable away from us. Excessive welfare programs diminish our ability and in our mind, the obligation to help. An even larger travesty, it kills the ambition of people who continuously get assistance to become self-reliant.

Yes, in a truly free society some will slip through the cracks. Yes, some will choose not to give to some people or some causes but this is the freedom we should retain. We should be free to choose how to distribute what we have earned while retaining the right to distribute nothing if we so choose. Some will not give anything which should be acceptable in a free society, should it not? Is the government so afraid if they do not *care* for the needy or less fortunate no one will? Is this really what they think of us? Proof of otherwise is rampant in America; we do help those in need despite government's interference. See my fish fry example. We may do it different and we may be unorganized *at first* but I would bet my money it would get done because I have trust and faith in the citizens of the United States. It would get done without the waste and without a permanent bureaucracy to oversee it. It should not be a bureaucrat or politician's job to tell us how charitable we should be. Anyone in government who demands a continuous program overseen by government is telling us something; they just do not think we the people are essentially good or trustworthy enough to do it on our own. Put simply, *they know better*.

If the government has the right to help the needy, it means they have the right to decide *who* is needy, *how* much they need, *who* needs to pay, *how* much they pay. It creates, maintains, and grows the endless additional intrusions by government. They will pit groups against other groups for benefits paid by the taxpayer. This will create ongoing political problems the likes of which we see in American society today. It is a system created deliberately to increase endless government involvement and meddling in our lives for it is the nature of government.

Chapter 8:   The Rightful Masters

A constant problem which may contribute to the potential faltering of a free society could be if the population is *too* comfortable. I think perpetual comfort for some people is detrimental. Comfort is an enemy. It breeds complacency. It breeds stagnation. In the United States of America historically speaking, human beings have never been as comfortable as they are here in America. Not a bad thing and I am glad to be a U.S. Citizen. To the high achiever, this comfort allows them to focus and achieve an even more fruitful life. On the other hand, to the fence sitter, comfort is a reason to think everything is fine and they may see no need to improve themselves but will still complain about not having everything someone else has.

Many people do not care about preserving freedom or taking risks to better themselves. Most Americans including me have no way to comprehend what it is like to live without the freedom we have always known. Some do not realize what they are giving up by relying on others or the government to take care of them. They do not realize how detrimental it is for them to wait to see what happens or for something good to happen to them. They do not realize how special and good the society they live in is because they have little interest in things which do not immediately benefit them. When people are fence sitters they do not realize how well they have it because they do not engage with enough focus to make the personal comparisons and see how they fit in.

87

They do not take the step which brings into light the one small additional piece of information which can make the big picture more understandable.

The success freedom has provided Americans as a whole is unrivaled to any in human history. The freedom to do as we wish in pursuit of our own desires and goals has afforded luxuries upon us regarding our lifestyle no other country has ever enjoyed. Our freedom begets us even more freedom when we are allowed to save and utilize the benefits of our labor later in life when the body is in need of retirement. We may choose to pool with others in the quest for growth of our money by providing such capital to others in need so they may make the same achievements. This is the beauty of Capitalism and I will discuss this more later.

Generations of success and desire to create or provide a better life especially after World War II has made life essentially a cake walk when compared to that of the 19th century. Extreme success when compared to the 1800's means the ability to feed, clothe, and shelter one's family without the reliance of others. I am not referring to the extreme rich who existed as they always have throughout history. I refer to the common man described and discussed so often today as middle class America. These Americans now live with a lifestyle never seen throughout times past societies. The everyday luxuries we enjoy today and have always known become the basic expectations for every following generation. We are now at a place where the next generation may not be able to enjoy a greater lifestyle and I believe it comes a great deal from an overly invasive government policy but also our inability to understand what it took to create this American lifestyle we enjoy.

A sense of entitlement especially over the past forty years has eroded the work ethic and industrious nature necessary to maintain and protect our way of life. When those values are not understood and taught as the driving force of successful Americans, a desire for the quick fix may cause an unhappy populace to forgo the very freedoms necessary for them to succeed. The more cornered they feel, the more dangerous an avenue they may be likely to choose. I fear we are at this crossroads now and without tremendous effort to explain and show how most people can succeed; our problem will only grow eventually to a point of no return.

We must explain why America is what it is, how it came about, and why it is so different than any other country in the world, why this is a good, and *not* something needing a *fundamental transformation*. The fact is if a majority does not understand the values and ideals which made America the greatest successful experiment in government and recognition of freedom, we shall surely lose said freedom. To lose the greatest opportunity ever to exist, that of being born a free citizen of the United States of America, all one has to do is nothing. A body and mind at rest tends to stay at rest. We must strive to be forever moving forward, learning, and being involved in our governance lest we leave decisions to those who may not act in our best interest.

We must as citizens take a personal oath and be aware of our duty to preserve, protect, and defend the Constitution of the United States. Cracks in the principled foundation of the Constitution cannot be allowed to form or expand. Finally when it is realized we have not lived up to our duty we must strive even harder to remedy the damages that may have occurred. We the People have not been diligent in this respect and we need to admit and correct it.

America and the American way of life have changed drastically in the way we have lived over the past two hundred years. We have such different daily tasks and the way we accomplish the tasks to meet basic needs has been made easier in so many ways, those who first came to America would never have imagined. This makes us more prosperous. I define prosperity in this context as having more free time as well as resources to pursue other activities outside of providing basic necessities. Today, we do not have to think about or deal with gathering food, cleaning and washing due to modern conveniences and technology. We do not have to worry as individuals about our neighbor next door going to war with us and laying siege to our home, I am very glad to say.

This will obviously influence human nature and lead to our thought process geared away from meeting basic necessities to more enjoyable activities. Although this makes for an easier life it can inevitably lead to stagnation of the mind. Our lives get filled with many activities which rob us of time but do not provide any material benefit to us other than entertainment. If this is our focus will we become a mass of people who like the Roman mob were interested in nothing more than bread and circuses? Is America too successful for those who are not do-ers? Does overall prosperity breed indifference in those who are fence-sitters? What do we need to do to make sure we are not wasting our prosperity on activities which do not improve ourselves and our minds? Indifference and inaction are not traits which made America great but they could be traits that negatively influence our society.

The Roman leaders knew they could make the population happy and compliant by simply giving them enough food and entertainment to occupy their time. The focus of these minimal needs and wants leads to the end of civilizations as was the case in the ancient Roman Republic. Eventually Rome fell and was over run by the barbarians from the north. I believe we are approaching the same problems in that *a society which does not actively focus on the increase of knowledge and understanding of reality and basic moral principles in its people - is doomed to mediocrity at its core.*

America is so great and so prosperous people have the luxury of not paying attention to what goes on outside their immediate family or bubble of influence. Our population is now too large and we must do even more now as do-ers to make up for the fence sitter who will never take action to preserve our freedoms but will only act if promised an immediate payback.

Being too comfortable also contributes to many of us not paying too much attention to what our legislators do to us. Most of us have no real concept of what hardship really is or could be unless you are old enough to remember World War II or served in that war. Only those in their eighties now can clearly remember those days or actually saw real hardship. From the baby boomer generation on there has been a boom in the United States and most of us have benefitted. I think part of the issue today stems from the disbelief real hardship the likes unseen since the Great Depression is a situation which cannot be repeated in the America of today. The Depression is merely pictures on TV seen by those who do not take the time to really understand the meaning of those pictures or more important, have any clue as to why it did happen.

Unfortunately it can happen again and may if we do not take control of our government to prevent the always unanticipated fallout from too much government intervention in the private affairs of the people. Some will never believe days such as those in the Depression can again return to America until they actually do. Then it is too late for reflection. I for one do not want to learn that costly lesson first hand but prefer to learn from history and our mistakes rather than be doomed to not only repeat them but even worse, to live them first hand. The cost of that lesson is too high for me and my family and the main reason for my writing of this book.

American ideals and freedoms are the exception in the long history of human beings. This is the one time in history where people were not ruled by a dictator or group but were recognized as having natural rights bestowed by their creator, and free to do as they will. We are still that exception, but it takes work to protect it. The Constitution is the tool but we must have virtuous and strong leaders to utilize it. We must do a better job.

We the people are the rightful masters of both Congress and the courts, not to overthrow the Constitution, but to overthrow the men who pervert the Constitution.
-Abraham Lincoln

I think we can easily agree Mr. Lincoln was a smart man and his statement here is correct if you believe in the Founding Fathers and the Constitution. The question is now: Is our Constitution being perverted? I say yes, it is obvious but my follow up question is:

Why do we allow it?

Another major reason why I think the internal drive of many is on average less than it was in the past is now, so many think they are entitled to *unearned greatness*. Now this is a concept I learned from James Taggert, a character in Ayn Rand's novel Atlas Shrugged. When I really understood what it meant, it was a revelation in my understanding of how too many people in society really think and how detrimental it can be to a society. When someone believes they should be revered, included, consulted with, and rewarded for doing absolutely nothing but *showing up* to earn such adulation, it appalls me and goes far against my way of thinking and I believe the American spirit. When this ugly trait in someone shows up, I cannot bare to see it.

Just as bad as the expectations of greatness for oneself are those who shower such admiration on those who do not earn it. For by doing this they are reinforcing their own beliefs that praise is something to give when positive results do not materialize or even before any actions are actually taken. This subject struck me and made me feel the need to write briefly about it because October 9, 2009 was the day we found out the Nobel Peace Prize was awarded to Barack Obama. This act strikes me directly as an act to promote unearned greatness by someone outside our country on our latest president. The decision was said to be based on his hope for a better future and nuclear disarmament. So, the Nobel Prize is awarded for hope? So recognition and praise are bestowed on someone because they *intend* to make things better by doing things *they* approve of? Nine months in office is enough time to decide if someone may have good intentions and should be rewarded according to the Nobel committee. This is not an American ideal and I guess it fits because it was awarded by Sweden, a very socialistic country. America's success is based on people getting things done.

The awarding of the Nobel Prize to Barack Obama goes against the ideals and values which make up the

American way or spirit. The American ideal is to be proud of what you achieved and the reward you attained for following through to make the accomplishment, big or small. We do not value with praise and tribute what someone may have in mind to do. We value what was done, what was created, the feat which was attained through hard work and determination. Although letting people know what you intend to do, which a good leader will, it is getting it done that really matters in the United States of America. Until then, it is nothing but immeasurable hype valued only as long as such rhetoric can be remembered.

If we get to a point where the only expectations of those in America is have an intention to succeed, the results will falter and the excuse of -*well you can not say I was not trying*- will become even more prevalent than it is today. It is the difference in saying you want to succeed and actually doing it which sets America apart from the rest of the world, and why it is the exception.

If I go to work everyday hoping I get something done but never do, will my boss reward me for my good intentions? Hell no, I'll be out on my rear fairly quickly and you know what? I should be! If I cannot earn the paycheck I receive by doing work which benefits my organization, why should they keep me?

The mentality of entitlement to anything and everything regardless of what was done to earn it really means this type of person has no respect for *your* effort, or *your* rights to your property. They will take it if they can get away with it and justify it with their good intentions.

What kind of country do we live in where doing and achieving something is not important, only the intent to achieve? I get a vision of a *commune* of people sitting around in a circle talking about what needs to happen, how things ought to be, how they feel about things, and what they intend to do tomorrow. When tomorrow comes they talk some more about what did not happen today and how important it is to do it. Meanwhile, no one is gathering food, repairing shelter, and feeding kids because they are talking about the best way to do these important things. Eventually one of the elders in the discussions said he was hungry and asked for some food so he could continue talking. It was then realized there was none. No one had planted anything the prior season because what kind of food to grow was still being discussed. They all died of starvation and deservedly so. The End.

It was the *assumption* there would always be *someone else* to provide food, which killed them. No one had done anything because if they had without approval, they would have been corrected or punished by the leaders. Also what food they may have produced illegally would have been taken as well to distribute as the leaders saw fit. So I conclude, in a damned if you do and a damned if you don't world, people would rather be damned if they don't.

Chapter 9: A Metamorphosis

Our government's job is not to take from some and give to others in the name of fairness, compassion, or benevolence. The government's job is to make and enforce laws which protect private property and provide the people the opportunity to prosper and to pursue happiness. It is not their job to try to guarantee it. Government should not create systems of regulation after regulation to keep tabs on us and meddle in our affairs. Joseph Ashby, writer for AmericanThinker.com wrote in an article entitled: *When Tyranny Calls* and said regarding politics in England, "No longer do politicians seek office as protectors of life, liberty, and property; they seek only to run the oppressive bureaucratic state more efficiently." It would be a short stretch to say this is true of most of our politicians in the United States today as well.

We are reaching a point where the growth of government is taking away our ability to take care of ourselves and those we care about. It has become oppressive in its continuous piling on of regulations and taxes and has indeed begun to make many citizens feel helpless. We work twice as hard and the government takes more from us. This increase in our time needed to support ourselves and our families leaves less and less time for the average U.S. Citizen to keep track of what the government does. I do not believe this to be anything but by design.

Government has grown and perverted its original purpose created by the Constitution. Many in government believe they have the right under the commerce clause or the general welfare clause of the Constitution to basically do as they please. This is a free country set up by our Founding Fathers and, by design this freedom does not ordain a few with the ability to infringe on the freedom of an individual, group, or entity for the sake of others. One of the main reasons for declaring independence was to *eliminate* the control of some by others who had no involvement other than a despotic need to meddle in the affairs of others.

People who have a natural tendency or need to tell others what to do are dangerous to our freedoms. They are drawn to government service because it is the only place in a free society where they get to fulfill their natural predisposition to dictate to others. The difference between these types of people and those in the private sector is when in government; they can get away with and thrive on these tendencies because they will not have to pay immediate consequences. Often large amounts of time pass before the real ramifications of their actions are known or understood. By then they are either out of the government office or other changes have occurred which were not originally contemplated, therefore direct blame is not placed on them or can be easily directed away from them.

In the private sector, results are evaluated much faster and corrective actions can take place to remove this type of person before irreversible damage occurs.

98

This does not happen in government. The private sector rewards or punishes results, government gets a pass on well intended policies even when it is proven better ideas were available and could have been used. There are people who will not pass judgment on anything lest they leave themselves open to the possibility of future criticism. They live with the fence sitting mindset where one must always find consensus with others before decisions are made. I agree consultation and discussions should be held to get better insight on ideas but in a way this gives insight into their thinking process when they want to continuously have discussions. They will never make a decision on their own when they can be part of the group think and share the blame if the decision turns out to be wrong. A true leader will listen to all the information available, consult with the experts if available, then make a decision and move forward.

We must confine ourselves to the powers described in the Constitution, and the moment we pass it, we take an arbitrary stride towards a despotic Government.
-James Jackson
First Congress

To promote the general welfare as stated in the Constitution does not give the government the right to seize people's freedom i.e. the fruits of their labor due to one easily construed statement. If it did, what would have been the purpose of the Constitution in the first place? Who in their right mind would have created a founding document as the basis to create a government, conceived in liberty and then completely undermine it by including language which renders it meaningless?

With respect to the two words "general welfare," I have always regarded them as qualified by the detail of powers connected with them. To take them in a literal and unlimited sense would be a metamorphosis of the Constitution into a character which there is a host of proofs was not contemplated by its creators.
-James Madison,
The Father of the Constitution

This reasoning by our representatives of using the general welfare clause as justification directly from the Constitution to do whatever they want is simply a blank check on our very lives with rules which apply in any fashion they choose. Common sense tells us this is not right but when said sense is as extinct as it seems to be now in government, we are all in peril of losing our liberty and freedom unless we put a stop to it. We cannot trust them anymore. We must know what goes on and stop back door and closed door dealings regarding legislation which affects us all. We need people who will go to congress and when they hear another speak of something secret or undermining, they immediately bring to the attention of the people and be damned of the fallout. Citizens will gladly follow a leader who shows this level of character and his seat would likely never come into question. Brutal but non-violent confrontation of those who would damage our republic should be the norm and not the exception. Only by exposing this flawed character and corruption of our government officials at the core, and relentlessly, will it be controlled and diminished. Those of weak character should fear being in Congress.

When the people fear their government, there is tyranny; when the government fears the people, there is liberty.

-Thomas Jefferson

This U.S. Citizen

Chapter 10: Trusted Leaders?

Why is it that it seems our government has the all knowing ability and right to oversee everything which goes on in the United States but it is the only entity rarely held accountable for mistakes? When so many are affected by government decisions, what sense does this make? Yes, we have the power to vote at election time but it rarely is enough to persuade the entire group to refocus on preserving the great aspects of our system. At elections the focus tends to be oriented toward a few high profile, polarizing, and always re-occurring issues in the effort to turn out just enough of the right votes to win. The focus is rarely if ever about giving us something to vote for versus voting for the lesser of two evils.

How can we, the citizens of the United States trust people who will not let us know what a bill actually says before they are passed? These so called legislators openly admit they do not understand legislative language and yet will pass a law like passing out lollipops without even knowing what flavor they are. Bills are written and influenced by lawyers, staffers, and lobbyists who could likely do little more than summarize the contents of the language let alone the potential consequences on the average U.S. citizen which will arise if passed into law. We have allowed people who have cheated on their *own* taxes to control our money and create tax laws. Would this have been tolerated one hundred years ago? Well, since there was no income tax one hundred years ago I guess that is a bad question but that is another topic in and of itself.

These are our *trusted* leaders in government and are allowed to set policy? Really, have we lost our minds to continue to allow this to happen? Would we knowingly put child molesters in charge of daycare centers? No! Then how do we get to a point where we allow these people to *rule* us like they do? This is what has changed: our government officials have taken on the mentality of rulers and ruling over the people instead of governing a system created for the direct benefit of every individual free citizen and *their pursuit* of happiness.

Once those who think they know better than us are in charge of us, they become bloated with the power they hold. The fact they truly believe we are below them intellectually makes them a danger and a menace to us and our freedoms. I fear we have reached that place and may have very little time remaining to redirect the government back to a system overseen by us instead of ruling over us by a poorly chosen few. Now that we have reached this point it is obvious our *rulers* do not understand what they are doing meaning we are ruled by very stupid and freedom ignorant people who think Freedom is an outdated concept or even worse, just another obstacle in their way. How many of our reps now advocate Freedom with any frequency? Very few unfortunately. It is time to change that!

Who do we put in government?

We must put only those in government who have the ability to make sound judgment calls and not yield under the pressure of those in government around them. We need people with backbone who are firm in their beliefs and not easily intimidated. We need people who do not go with the flow, which is what most do because it is *easy*. We need reps and senators who are different, who will fight and be ok with being targets of the opposition. We need those who will not compromise the Constitution by making closed door deals with other politicians whose idea of governing is supporting each others' ideas merely to get their own passed.

Our form of government created by the Constitution cannot be left to be preserved by wishy washy and indecisive people who will change their minds often and go with whichever way the wind blows and is politically expedient. The Constitution is not a living document in my opinion but is the equivalent of bedrock for our nation. It is the foundation with which everything depends. We cannot build and grow a better United States if the starting point is not firmly seated in said bedrock. The notion of the Constitution as a living document is simply a statement which pre sells to people the idea that it is ok to make drastic changes to it as time passes. It is certainly not.

Technology and industries have changed in two hundred years but not to a point if there could ever be a point which would justify a continuous usurping of the basic tenets of the Constitution. The foundation is not perfect but it is sound; the most sound of any society in history. We must only send those people to government who are also *sound* and of the ability to make good judgments based on the Constitution as their oath of office requires.

Unfortunately, upholding the Constitution today is at most second on our government officials' list of importance. We should know we are in a bad state when the Speaker of the House is asked if she thinks a certain piece of legislation is Constitutional and she responds with "is that a serious question." We are indeed reaching the end of our rope. The fact this attitude exists at such a high level in our government is appalling to me.

Re-election I fear is the number one focus for those in our government now due in part to ignorance of their role in government and having been taken over by human nature when surrounded by those who also aspire to maintain their power positions as long as possible and at nearly any cost. If indeed re-election is the main goal then our reps will not address an issue first and foremost as to whether it is permissible under the Constitution and/or detrimental to the freedoms of individual citizens. Instead it is reviewed with consideration as to *how the public will perceive the legislation*. What they worry about is whether the public will like or dislike his *support* of the issue and therefore how voters will act come election time. This is downright cowardly leadership in my book.

It is a total disregard of their oath of office in my opinion but it is what takes place. I would venture to say if they held strictly to the Constitution, not only would a lawmaker's job be easier, so would their election. Is this not a reasonable conclusion I ask? If not, then is it an issue of the peoples' understanding of our government and the Constitution? The education of our peers is our responsibility to correct this issue. This is part of our duty as citizens to protect and defend our republic from its destruction from within.

What is their job?

This U.S. Citizen gets the distinct impression our representatives and senators do not see themselves as in congress to represent the people in their district or state. They are there to be *fixers*. They consider themselves to have a mandate by election on solving problems *they* think are important and work toward those goals once in office. This disconnect is what I believe to be another major reason why the Congress approval rates are so low in 2009 and early 2010. When we continuously see our officials on television talking about what they think is important and blatantly ignoring the obvious will of the people, it is personally insulting to me.

The superficial tactic they use when trying to rally support for their goals is communicated with the simple phrase: *"The American people want this"* or *"The American people need that."* These are cheap salesman tactics which play on the individual and make them think other Americans must want this so I must be out of touch if I don't support it as well. This then kicks in the herd mentality to follow the reps statements and take them as facts when they are not. The same applies when they say *"Americans deserve..."* for example: good medical care or good schools.

Americans do not *deserve* anything! We work for what we have. You *deserve* what you work for, period! When you buy into the notion of Americans *deserving anything* because it is supposedly the right thing to do, you buy into the reps definitions of what good medical care is and what a good school is. The problem is they get to define *good.* What is good for the rep or senator is not necessarily good for the individual U.S. Citizen. A good idea can stand on its own and is easily understood as well as easily communicated. If they are good ideas, bring them to the spotlight and explain why they are necessary and what will be the likely results of such ideas if implemented. If an idea cannot be explained in a simple and straightforward manner with a reasonable and logical argument, it is more likely to not be good for the United States or its citizens. Is that too much to ask?

I think our officials do not feel they are obligated to talk to us unless election time is near. I really believe *they think we are stupid.* We must admit when it comes to politics, civics, and safeguarding our country and freedoms, we have some work to do. It is to their benefit we stay that way because it allows them to do as they please and keep their jobs to boot. Well I say no more. I hope we have had enough of this attitude from our government. The fact is, they are not good at what they do and there are numerous examples to prove it.

They create policies with so called good intentions which eventually lead to horrendous problems. They want to keep us uninformed because a well informed and educated electorate is a danger to them and their government plans. They give more money to schools where there is proof more money does not improve results. Just look at the Washington DC schools! They support teacher unions and vice versa where the interest is in the growth of the unions and pay of the teachers, not the education of children. They control the curriculum and dumb it down where a student will not feel bad due to his otherwise poor performance on a normal curriculum. They advance failing students to the next grade because they do not know how to educate them where the students' self esteem will be degraded even further because the work is harder for them when they could not even do last year's work. This is the kind of outcome which emerges from poorly done legislation enacted by people who are rarely accountable and care only about what an issue can do for their political career.

When our reps and senators have to disguise what they are doing by saying it is too complicated and will not allow legislative language to be reviewed by the public and understood, we can rest assure they are up to no good and are likely attempting to hijack our freedoms.

This was ever present in the reform of our medical system taking place in the fall of 2009 and early 2010.

When our reps do not represent the will of their constituents and actually and blatantly ignore their concerns and desires, this is no longer the representative republic our founders created. So Benjamin Franklin's statement remains relevant today. Can we indeed keep our Republic?

I heard a Fox News commentator in October, 2009 named Tammy Bruce and I think what she said is very relevant and applies directly to our Congress and representatives. She said, "*Justice only occurs when people are looking.*" It is sad we live in a country where this is true. We have to send people to government who are trustworthy enough to do *our* business and not have to constantly watch over them every minute of every day. We may however have to do that very thing for the next few years or few election cycles.

When it comes to sending people to Congress or any form of government, we need to use the viewpoint I learned from a management professor I know. She said when it comes to hiring, *hire people you do not have to manage.* I think there is a bit of genius in that philosophy. We need to use this same philosophy in choosing our government officials.

Chapter 11:   Morally Treasonable

It's our fault we have waited this long. It's our fault we have not stood up for American exceptionalism and passed down those traits which make America great. In order to get things done we have to have the backbone to tell those who are wrong, they are wrong, give the facts, and move on. Many times those who are wrong do not want to accept it so they push back. The push back is where sometimes I think we falter. We do not like confrontation and those who are wrong may not take it well when pointed out by others so they raise a raucous and in the past we have backed down. It is time for that to stop. One person who might be wrong or offended by something should not be able to control an important conversation.

How did we get to a point in a country where our rights including the right to freedom of religion which is protected by the Constitution is being changed to something more like freedom *from* religion? Christmas trees are now offensive and cannot be put in public places because one person is offended. How is this rational? Having freedom of religion does not mean it gives you the right that you will not see it around you, less you be offended. This mentality is just petty, and so are those people.

This mentality I think comes from people being so scared to say what is right or wrong because someone will take offense and is inherent in the reason behind the statement saying it is best not to talk about religion or politics. It is time we started talking about these things and get past the awkwardness so we can face and understand the real issues in these areas. We only solve problems when we address them clearly, based on facts, and not controlled by emotion. Supporting or joining a political party and simply supporting without questioning the authority, the reasoning, and facts is detrimental to our way of life. Everyone at *all levels* should be criticized and questioned and often.

> *To announce that there must be no criticism of the president, or that we are to stand by the president, right or wrong, is not only unpatriotic and servile, but is morally treasonable to the American public.*
> -Theodore Roosevelt

In 2009 we had a president who took an oath to protect and defend the Constitution of the United States. This president stated on Chicago public radio in 2001 that quote "the Constitution was a charter of negative liberties. Says what the states can't do to you. Says what the federal government can't do to you, but doesn't say what the federal government or state government must do on your behalf."

Now answer me this question, how can someone fulfill the oath to the Constitution if he does not understand that the Constitution was created to protect people *from* an oppressive government when his whole goal is to do things *to* people or do things *on our behalf*? His basic assumption is not only backward but insulting to me in that he thinks we want and need things done for us, let alone *to* us. So what is it he thinks the government must do that the Founding Fathers were so ignorant they obviously overlooked in 1787? I would like to know, wouldn't you? It is my understanding these so called negative liberties imposed on the federal government are essentially permanent handcuffs on the government to prevent it from controlling the people and everything we do. It seems the current administration has unlocked the handcuffs with the assistance of the Congress and has revoked these negative liberties to achieve their goals, whatever they might be!

We can no longer trust, at least for the next few decades, those who have been trusted with the power of our government. The government exists of the people, by the people, and for the people. It is time we the people enforced this notion again. As stated in the Constitution; the government can only act with the consent of the governed. Do you feel like you have been giving your consent regarding what the government has done in the past few decades? I certainly do not.

When we as parents create and enforce rules on our children, it is done because we actually *do* know what is best for them based on our experiences, our beliefs, and our culture. We know they do not possess the knowledge or experience necessary to properly weigh risks and costs involved in their actions so we take actions limiting these risks and costs on them as well as on us, the parents. This is the same approach I believe our government uses to justify what they do to us; fully grown United States Citizens. The problem for them is that *we are not their children*! We should not be bound to whatever rules they decide to put upon us based on their supposed superior knowledge and their perceived lack of ability to make proper decisions for ourselves. When they do this year after year they are essentially boxing in free people, making our lives more and more confining with the expectation we will grow accustomed to their changes and life will go on. What they fail to realize is people accustomed to freedom will take this kind of treatment for a long time. However a point will be reached where people will refuse to be boxed in and controlled any further. How far away is this tipping point? I believe with the emergence of the tea party movement in 2009 and the contempt shown toward citizens by many representatives, we just might be there.

The day I wrote this particular paragraph was Jan. 12, 2010 and I, a Texan just made my first monetary contribution to an out of state election candidate. It was to Scott Brown, the MA Senate candidate in an effort to do what I could to end the supermajority in the senate which existed at that time to possibly derail the current administrative agenda and stop the healthcare takeover. He went on to defeat his opponent I am glad to say. We will have wait and see if Mr. Brown is worthy of the position we have given him or if indeed we once again chose the lesser of two evils.

The actions of our government today, the state of the economy, and the security threats which exist have in my opinion, nationalized the concerns of this U.S.

Citizen. I have faith I am not the only citizen who has come to this conclusion.

What is the role of our government?

I believe the United States Government should be a *partner*, not a parent of the people. It should not be a provider for some citizens at the expense of other citizens. The terrible approval numbers prove this currently is how the government is viewed by the majority of citizens. My thoughts of our government when it takes actions are in terms of wondering just how negative their latest legislative venture will affect me because the positive aspects as touted rarely emerge. The policies created by government rarely create outcomes which make me happy but rather create more uncertainty in my life. To exist in a permanent state of uncertainty is no way for free people to live and yet this is where we find ourselves today.

What would it feel like to have representatives, a congress, and entire government we could trust to do what is right regarding creating opportunities in the context of protecting our freedoms instead of protecting their positions of power? One can only wish I am afraid to say. Protecting our freedom can no longer be a spectator sport by the citizens of the United States. Active and permanent participation as the duty of citizenship must become the norm if we are to maintain the liberty we enjoy.

One of the other problems with current government is in order for them to push the need to create more laws and regulations, they must continuously push the notion things are bad in America. I am sad to say this tactic works. We are many times lulled into believing a crisis exists because we hear it day after day. The lawmakers release statements to the press which are repeated on today's continuous news cycles. Eventually we get tired of hearing it, tune it out, and try to worry about ourselves and stop paying attention. Again I think this is how we are taken advantage of. Lawmakers have all day everyday to come up with new ideas to pursue while we try to earn a living everyday and have scarce time to watch over them. We work to feed our families and to support the lawmakers' ideas and programs with our taxes. Well, it is really the other way around because they take our earnings first for their ideas through tax withholding and payroll taxes then we get what is left for our families.

The way of thinking lawmakers have when it comes to our earnings appalls me. When a tax cut is talked about, those in government who oppose it say it is too much of a cost. *A cost to whom?* If someone thinks of letting people keep more of *their* earnings as a cost to them, what does it say about how they think of all of our earnings? They approach it from a stance where *all* of our earnings is theirs to do with what they please. They are inclined to take as much as they can up to the point where people will not see it as worth it anymore to work. This is how they have control of us and it is not right.

The government drives the people in *its* desired direction by rewarding or punishing citizens' action through the use of the Income Tax Code. The Founding Fathers in 1787 did not give the Congress the power to tax our incomes which remained the case until in 1913 when that was changed with the 16th Amendment. Less than 100 years of taxes on our income and I ask, are we a better, more opportunistic nation because of this?

It is not right to force us through the use of the tax code to do what they happen to feel is right on a whim year after year. The more we have to work to make up for what they take from us, the less time we have to pay attention to what the are doing. It is a vicious cycle the Founding Fathers would never have supported. Fact is, they did not support taxing the incomes of the citizens. This change came about in 1913 along with creating a central banking system, which was vehemently opposed to by Thomas Jefferson during his time. This central banking system called the Federal Reserve controls the cost and price of money by interest rates and by having total control over the country's currency. This is central planning and price fixing within our monetary system. Although the *Federal Reserve* in name sounds like it is part of the government, it is not. It is a totally *private* banking entity which works in secret in pursuit of its own interests, not the interests of the citizens of the U.S. The Fed as it is called does not disclose its actions to anyone, even the Congress of the United States. 1913 also saw the change in how Senators are chosen by taking the choice away from the state governments in lieu of direct elections. This drastically reduced the power of the states in relation to keeping the federal government in check. 1913 was a very bad year for citizens' freedom but very good for creating more levers of control over the people by the government.

The privately-owned Central Bank is an institution of the most deadly hostility existing against the principles and form of our Constitution... if the American people allow private banks to control the issuance of their currency, first by inflation and then by deflation, the banks and corporations that will grow up around them will deprive the people of all their property until their children will wake up homeless on the continent their fathers conquered.
-Thomas Jefferson

Chapter 12: The Natural Progress

As time passes and as government grows, the more it takes from us so the less we as individuals are left to deal with. The human mind can do wonderful things and learn a great deal but if the challenges in life have been *solved* by the government, what are we left to do? By the act of trying to do everything for us they are condemning us to over reliance on the government and killing individualism. Is it on purpose? This is not good for the soul of America and I think can only lead to stagnation of the mind and therefore of the country. We need challenges and we need to figure things out for ourselves. When we do, we grow our confidence and self esteem and feel good about ourselves having cleared life's hurdles on our own. If problems are solved for us, what does that leave our minds to do? The word *solved* being a very weak word here because I do not think a government bureaucracy is capable of solving problems, only exacerbating them.

A system which subsidizes too long someone who is having difficulty only lengthens the time where they would find a solution for themselves. Government prevents growth and inhibits innovation for the sake of compassion. Is it compassionate to keep people in a state of anxiety? Yes it will be hard but left alone, a good person will find a way. They will make changes in their life but not as long as they have the permanent government teat to run back to when there is a bump in the road. People should fall back on family, community, or their church, and not on a permanent government program.

When I say a *good person*, I mean someone who will get their hands dirty and do what it takes legally to succeed. A criminal will cheat and steal and there will always be those who work that way. This is one of the necessities of government. To catch and punish those who cheat the system thereby making it safe for the rest of us to live lawfully. I am more than glad to pay my share of taxes for this role of government. The problem is that government does not know when to stop. The mere fact our so called representatives sit in Washington makes them think they should be doing something which leads to more government intervening in our lives. I believe this is a fault with our government and should be addressed potentially by having shorter legislative sessions or possibly term limits. They just have too much time on their hands and feel they need to do something to justify their next election.

Since I mentioned term limits, let me take a moment to put in my two cents worth. Term limits would be a good idea as an initial thought, but what would it do? I think it might just give us, the people one more reason to not pay attention to our government officials. We already have the ability through elections to make a House member or Senator a one term official, but we don't! That simply needs to change instead of focusing on term limits. To get term limits changed, the representatives and senators have to write a bill about the potential problems they themselves might create. Do you really think they are going to do that? Be self critical, a politician? Doubtful.

What does need to change is how our senators are chosen as I discussed briefly before. Originally senators were appointed by state legislators per the Constitution instead of by popular vote. This changed in 1913 by the 17th Amendment making popular vote the method of choosing Senators. Oddly this was the same year only two months and five days earlier the 16th Amendment passed giving Congress the power to tax our incomes. Hmm…

Although on the surface this sounds like a freer way to choose but the Founding Fathers were not fools. The reason they were to be appointed by the state legislators was to keep them under control of the people of each state and not subject to the whims of a federal government. Because of this I think people are less involved in their state governments because they see little reason to be. Any effect from not being involved in state government is difficult to understand when trying to relate it to their personal situation. So today, senators are not extensions of or a voice of the states any longer as intended but are only accountable to a majority of people who can be swayed to vote for them every six years. This I believe was a move to a mob rule or democracy mentality and to consolidate federal influence on future elections. It was a move away from the representative republic the Founding Fathers so carefully crafted.

Just a side note, the word democracy does not appear in the Constitution because the Founding Fathers wanted no part of a society based on mob rule, which is the definition of a true democracy. For example, we have laws against murdering other people. If you murder someone, you broke the law and you will be punished. It would be a travesty to change the law to make murder legal. We know it would not be right. That is why we are supposed to send only very trusted lawmakers to Congress and throw them out if they falter. This is a system which keeps us safe. Laws are made by 535 highly trusted people to represent the people and signed into law by a trusted president. Then the law if contested is reviewed by the Supreme Court to assure the law is Constitutional. Those on the Supreme Court are chosen by the sitting president. This again shows the importance of having a president who has been properly vetted, is understood to be of sound character, and believes wholeheartedly in the Constitution *as written and the patriots who drafted it*. If a true democracy existed where every person's vote was used to create laws, he who could sway 51% of the voters could do anything. With 51% of the vote, murder could be made legal. This is how a true democracy works and why it was avoided by the Founding Fathers completely. So whenever I here someone say we live in a democracy, it makes me cringe because I know they really do not know what are talking about.

When our representatives and senators think and act as if they know what is best for us, it is time to take action by the citizenry. Our opinions have been cast aside in lieu of an overriding agenda. The only time when our opinion matters is when elections are at hand, which they soon will be. Even then these officials seem to focus on a goal of trying to sway opinion to win an election instead of merely doing what is right for the country. I wonder if they think there is a difference in the two. It is our duty to participate, to be informed, and to be in control of our government. If we do not get involved, we affirm the actions of those who will increase governmental power, increase taxes, and over burden the people with excessive bureaucracy. It is again the very nature of government. The decline of freedom is inherent in these actions.

Those who believe they know better than you have no interest in consulting with or listening to you. When your leaders get to a point where they believe listening to their constituents is a hindrance to their legislative or party goals, this is an example of the ultimate in arrogance of our government. To them it is a waste of their time. Those in charge of our government and those in Congress have now reached this point. *The problem for them is we now realize it as a fundamental issue and a danger to our freedom and our republic.* When it is the case that consulting with constituents is not part of the process of governance, the necessary oversight and accountability of government by the people is eliminated. The streamlining of power held by elected officials begins to run amuck. Such is the state of our government today.

Government Spending

Why is government spending and a large deficit so bad for America? I think many people hear these words and this question but may not really understand the implication of high spending and bloated deficit spending. I will admit I did not really understand it until a few years ago but that came with paying close attention to what the government is doing and by reading. We continuously hear our reps talk about the deficit and how the deficit is bad and people will agree but, when you ask them why, rarely can you get a consistent answer. Well if I could I would like to use this opportunity to try to clarify what happens when the government spends money.

For one thing, when the government spends money it must first *take* money from somewhere. The government does not have *any* money to spend. When they spend money, they must take it from us, the citizens or they must borrow it. They take our money by taxing us. Just see the withholdings on your most recent paycheck stub for proof. The government takes our money and spends it on things *they* believe are necessary and more important to the point it takes our money before we ever see it, thus preventing our use of it. Just a quick question: can you imagine how mad people would be if they really understood how large their tax bill was by having to actually write a check for the entire amount every April? Instead the government has changed the frame of mind of *paying* our taxes into looking forward to getting a refund because they took too much of your money from you. They used your money and paid you no interest for borrowing it. The government likes no cost loans and they take them from us every year and yet we do nothing about it. I will discuss a solution to this tax issue later in this book.

Now regarding government spending, when the government spends our money they inhibit our ability to utilize that money for the uses we desire. No consideration is ever given on the real cost of taxes when it come to reducing economic activity stimulated by the free individual and the use of his money as he sees fit. The focus is always geared toward an immediate need usually in some area which stimulates emotions in people. When decisions are based on emotions instead of facts, potential consequences, and the likelihood of mistakes increase. Need proof? Look at all the programs created by government and tell me one which is run efficiently and effectively after an honest assessment and then tell me would they be worth repeating. I cannot think of any. The reality is those in government spend our money in such inefficient and wasteful ways because they are not held accountable for mistakes. It is very easy and I am sure quite intoxicating to be elected to spend other peoples' money and receive a paycheck for doing it as well. Don't you think?

The spending of Americans' money has now been so intoxicating to our government officials it is now reached a point where our standard of living is about to begin declining if it hasn't already. Our taxes are increasing to cover government's needs and our ability to borrow money from other countries is diminishing. Countries such as China have now in 2010 started reducing the amount of US debt it holds because it is worried about their investments. They are worried our financial system could have more and even greater problems in the future thereby putting their holdings at risk. Understanding risk as a financial person myself, I would be worried about my money too, and I am.

The Federal Reserve has created so much money now and inflated the dollar to the point other countries feel it is too risky to hold the dollar and in 2009, new reserve currencies were beginning to be discussed. This also causes these countries to not be interested in buying our bonds (i.e. loaning us money) because they know they will be repaid with dollars which are less valuable in the future. To pay the interest alone on our federal debt is costing us billions every single year. This is money which is buying us nothing but time while worsening economic activity is impeding our very ability to earn more money and thereby pay more taxes. It is a spiraling effect.

Eventually we will have to pay back the principal of the money we have borrowed. Where are we ever going to get that kind of money? To use an analogy most people understand, the U.S. is now much like a person who has maxed out their credit cards and cannot even afford to pay the minimum payment. Every day the debt load gets higher and higher and none of our money goes toward trying to lower our debt load by paying on the principal. Lowering the debt and government spending will keep our creditors happy and prove to them we are financially responsible and not close to bankruptcy. The creditors of the United States are not happy with us right now.

You see, if others believe we can not pay our debt back, they will attempt to do the prudent thing we would all do and cut their losses. This means any dollars they currently hold, they will try to get rid of by purchasing goods, commodities, food, as well as other currencies used throughout the world. They will try to get rid of their dollars because they fear they will become of lesser value or worthless very soon. This flooding of the market with dollars to purchase everything in sight will cause extreme demand and additional fear in others who hold U.S. dollars. What this leads to eventually and very quickly is the skyrocketing of prices of everything priced in dollars. This avalanche is caused because as people want to get rid of their dollars, less people want to take dollars due to the high risk of a U.S. bankruptcy. So in order for someone to take dollars for goods, they will demand more dollars to hedge *their* risk of now holding the declining U.S. dollar.

This is the dreaded hyperinflation scenario which can be caused by government overspending, borrowing, an out of control federal deficit, and excessive taxes. In essence, the money and savings you may have saved your entire life could be made essentially worthless and you can do nothing about it. This is the ultimate price and it will be paid by you and me, the citizens of the United States if we do not start getting control of our government. Is this a good enough reason to start paying attention to what is going on in Washington and what our government is doing to us with their extremely excessive spending?

Something else really bothers me about how our government goes about spending the money it takes from us. Now there are legitimate needs for government where funds are necessary such as in the defense of the nation and the people against its enemies but I am not talking about that particular issue. It is a fact that government sees fit to attempt to socially engineer our behavior through its programs and to influence how we live by punishment and reward. They attempt to steer us into taking actions that benefit them and their power. This is done for example by giving tax incentives to buy certain cars, car they want us to drive. What right do they have to punish me into driving the car they want? It is not authorized by the commerce clause or the welfare clause as we have already discussed.

Another problem for which we are stuck with the bill is when the government creates its programs *for our benefit* using our tax dollars. They many times create them to last forever and also build in automatic increases in funding which will add more to the program every year, growing additional government without actually making new laws. For example and this may get a little numbers heavy, but such is my nature and may be another silly example but it does make a good point. Let us say a law is written to spend $100 per year on widgets (a fictional government need), and the study of widgets effect on the ph level of interior wall paint used by U.S. citizen homeowners. Feel free to add as many zeros on to that $100 as you like, the government seems to and again bear with me here with a silly example but remember we are talking about government spending here. So, in the creation of the law it is determined there will always be a need for this program and it will need funding forever. It is also determined because the population is expected to grow every year and inflation must of course be considered, the funding for the widget wall paint ph program's funding must increase by 3% per year for five years then by 7% every year after. Wow, on a side note, this is a pretty good deal for those widget makers and those who study widgets. They will be happy to support their representative with money and votes for this measure and also unlikely to vote for him if he does not. Although it was not my intention here to show how elections are influenced, I think this makes it quite clear.

Once a program like this is in place, anyone saying spending in this area should be cut will be accused of not caring about the poor widget employee who will lose their job in that congressional district, especially that district's congressman. Part of this point is programs continue for reasons which go way beyond those for which they were originally established.

Now to return to my point regarding spending or spending cuts once a program is in place. To you and I, when we cut spending in our households, it means quite simply; we spend less money than we did before, correct? If we are spending $100 per month on eating out and our spending goes to $75 per month, this is a reduction in spending in our eating out budget. Well, the government does not work that way. In many cases, a so called cut in spending is merely a reduction, usually temporary, in the automatic yearly increase which is built in when the program was created. Let us go back to the widget example and it is now ten years since the program went into effect. Due to the automatic increase of 3% for five years and 7% thereafter, we are now spending $162.59 in year ten on the program. Please note, a financial calculator is helpful here! So a program sold to the public by politicians which cost the U.S. citizens $100 at inception is now costing us $162.59 this year thanks to built in automatic increases. That is ten years into the program and the automatic increase is now 7% per year so we can expect to spend $173.98 next year in year eleven. Just a quick question, is it any wonder the federal budget is so large when they use this kind of math?

Okay, so hypothetically let's assume the government decides it needs to cut some spending, so how do they do it? Well, in many cases they simply cut the automatic increase. Rarely if ever do they reassess and/or eliminate unnecessary programs completely. So in this case they reduce the automatic increase from 7% to say 6.45% so instead of spending $173.98 next year, they spend a mere $173.08. Remember last year in year ten of this example, $162.59 was spent and next year $173.08 will now be spent thanks to the money saving cut in spending. So technically, the government will spend *less than was originally expected* but in reality, they still spent much more than last year. And now you know how a politician can say he voted for spending cuts but in reality still without much notice, voted to spend more on the program in the following year. This is nothing more than taking advantage of built in wiggle room created by politicians so they can have their cake and eat it too. They can tout a spending cut to the voting public but still increase funding to the widget maker so as to continue their support for his reelection as well.

If you and I cut spending in our personal households this way, we would be bankrupt. I guess it is somehow okay to work math this way when you are spending other peoples' money, our money, the money which belongs to the U.S. Citizens who actually earn it.

The natural progress of things is for liberty to yield and government to gain ground.
-Thomas Jefferson

This U.S. Citizen

Chapter 13: Enlighten the People

In a way, this U.S. Citizen believes those currently in our government think they are the owners and controllers of our bodies and what that body produces. This is certainly evident when those in government speak regarding taxes and costs. When you hear a legislator who is against cutting taxes for ordinary citizens or businesses, they often refer to this as a *cost* to the government and that it will increase deficits. I would say only those with the mentality that considers our money as being their property in the first place would refer to its loss of use to the government as a cost. Someone of this mindset is not a servant of the people. This has a built in assumption that all our money is potentially theirs except what they deem acceptable for us to keep. Federal income tax withholding goes one step further down this path because the government does indeed take what they want first and we get the remainder in our *net* paycheck.

Here we are today; at a point where a tax cut to the people that earn the money is viewed as a cost or a negative action by the government. It may be a negative to the government, but it is a positive to the freedom of the people.

This U.S. Citizen has been trying to think of ways which can help to open the eyes of the American people as to the view of us by our government and how they run our lives and businesses. This U.S. Citizen can think of one way which will quickly encourage citizens to get involved in their government's oversight. It involves a relatively simple action which will focus the attention directly on the disconnect between our representatives and the citizens who send them to Washington. What I propose is to eliminate the withholding of our money for federal income taxes from *all* the citizens' paychecks.

Why would this help you may ask? Well let me just say I have a bumper sticker on my vehicle which says "FEDERAL INCOME TAX WITHHOLDING, A TEMPORARY WARTIME MEASURE SINCE 1943." The withholding tax was sold to the public as a wartime emergency and a national necessity, but like most government programs, it just never ended. The consequence of the withholding tax is that it took most of the burden, the calculation of, the pain of, and in that, *the very understanding* of how much each of us pay in income taxes every year.

On several occasions I have seen many strange looks on people's faces when they read that statement on my bumper sticker. They look very confused. I myself did not really understand the withholding of federal taxes and how it worked until I was a personal financial advisor working with families regarding their saving efforts and money management. I would say 95% of the people I helped did not understand their taxes. Doing federal taxes meant nothing much more to them than putting numbers into a tax program and printing a return to mail or dropping off boxes of paper and receipts to their tax preparer in the hope they did not have to pay in this year. As their advisor, my job was to try to help them create a budget, track, and possibly improve their monthly cash flows in their households. This meant making it easier for them to pay bills, save for retirement, and most important for those with kids or newborns, to save for their future college education.

The first place I always looked for ways to improve monthly cash flow for people was looking at their last few years of tax returns. What I began to notice and was a very consistent finding was about 95% of people had a history of receiving relatively large refunds due to them after filing their federal taxes every year. For single people, I would say the average refund was around $1,500 if I remember correctly and this was occurring in years 1999-2005. But what struck me was the refund most married people received and especially if they had children. I would say the average was $3,000 or more easily. My next step was to ask them what they would normally do with their refund money. A few said they saved it but the majority used it as *fun money*. They would use it for vacation or just spend a large portion of it. Most would use it for something they honestly told me they did not really need but for something they wanted and suddenly had the means to obtain. Human nature took over and the ability to satisfy an immediate want trumped better judgment. It happens to all of us!

After this discussion I would then tell them something which gave me again those same confused looks I get when people read my bumper sticker. I would ask them this: "Do you know when you get such a large tax refund such as this in fact what you have essentially done is given the federal government an interest free loan of your money over the past year? And if you had that money on a monthly basis you could have earned the interest by having it in a bank or saved it for your other financial goals helping you reach them possibly a little sooner?" Again I would receive a look which said they now understood how they had been for all intents and purposes, swindled out of the *use of their money* for the past year. It was always a revelation to them.

They would ask me what to do about it and I would then help them understand how to adjust their withholdings with their employers. It really is very easy and most people had no idea they could even do this or how. This was a clear and very prevalent lack of understanding of how our tax system currently works. *A U.S. Citizen should not be this disarmed of the knowledge of how its government uses them as a resource for government endeavors.* All you have to do is fill out a W-4 form from the IRS website and give it to your payroll department. By law they must make the change immediately and your next paycheck will reflect the difference, giving you the ability to use your money now instead of waiting until filing taxes the following year.

Now why did I go through this explanation? Because it illustrates the disconnect the ordinary U.S. citizen has with the amount of tax dollars they really pay and how the government and Congress spends our money. By withholding peoples taxes from their paycheck before they ever see it, people do not *feel* the pain of their tax bill. Our government has created a system where our money is taken from us and most Americans think of doing their taxes as a positive thing for them because when they do file in the spring every year, they get a big monetary payoff. A little bit of that *immediate gratification* discussed earlier. We actually feel good about getting ripped off by our government but most do not even know they were swindled.

I admit it works and there are today only a small percentage of the U.S. taxpayers who really understand this. The proof is evident by asking anyone you know a simple question. Ask them this: "How much did you pay in federal income taxes last year?" Nine times out of ten I bet the answer you receive will be along the lines of: "I didn't have to pay, I got money back!" This response tells you there is no real understanding of what they pay in taxes every year of their working lives.

Now to go back to my recommendation of eliminating all the withholding for federal income taxes from paychecks and what it would do. But first, just to be understandable, I am not advocating here eliminating income taxes, the IRS, or changing rates of any sort. I'm simply talking about eliminating the withholding tax from our paychecks in this particular instance. Discussing rates and the income taxes overall is another book altogether.

So what would it do? Yes, it would create some problems for some but what it would do is create tremendous focus on the government *by the taxpaying U.S. citizens*. It would return to the citizen the

137

responsibility of tracking, budgeting for, and actually paying the income tax bill. When the citizen must actually write a very large check to the IRS in the spring instead of getting back their no interest loan they gave to the government, more citizens *will* take notice of how much they pay in taxes. They will not be happy.

People would suddenly become very interested in the spending done by our federal government because they would actually feel the cost burden put on them by their representatives and senators. When we live under a system where the taxpayer does not understand their role in paying for government and our representatives are allowed to spend this tax money (ours) at will, our entire system and country is in trouble. This type of system breeds corruption. There is no accountability because lawmakers are only accountable at elections by voters. The American voter cannot hold them accountable because the facts and understanding of the true costs involved are obfuscated due to the government by a system that keeps them in the dark.

My suggestion is to repeal the federal withholding for income taxes for U.S. Citizens and watch as a *revolution of understanding* emerges.

Enlighten the people, generally, and tyranny and oppression of body and mind will vanish like spirits at the dawn of day. ...If a nation expects to be ignorant-and free- in a state of civilization, it expects what never was and never will be.
-Thomas Jefferson

Chapter 14:   Evils of Capitalism?

Evils of Capitalism and Job Creation

Capitalism seems to be getting a bad rap these days and I cannot understand why but I have come to believe many do not understand what true capitalism is and how it works. It is my understanding the capitalist system is the only way to increase our standard of living and has done so since the founding of this nation. Where else in the world are the poorest people able to afford cars, the latest cell phones, flat screen television sets, cheap food, hundred dollar sneakers, etc.? It is due directly to the results of Capitalism.

Capitalism simply promotes free trade between parties. One party or entity creates a product to sell and sets a price. Another person, party or entity may need the product and is willing to pay a certain price. If the price is agreeable, the trade occurs and both parties are happy and move on. If the seller sells the product for more than it cost to produce the product, that is the profit. The profit is where the *capital* in Capitalism is formed. If he cannot sell the product for more than it cost to produce it, he is out of business or needs to improve his ability to produce the product at a lower cost. It is as simple as that.

This capital created from the profit is then used to improve the business by researching improvements making the product better and more attractive to buyers creating more sales of the product. This expands the operation which leads to more jobs for more people. This still is a good thing is it not? Is *this* the evil of Capitalism? Also the capital or profit allows the product through research or streamlining to be made cheaper and thereby sold for a cheaper price. This makes it more affordable to a greater number of people which improves standard of living. It gives a person's income the ability to purchase more goods which may have in the past been luxury items, for example, the flat screen televisions of today. Remember when flat screen televisions first appeared at costs to a buyer of tens of thousands of dollars and in 2009 could be purchased for hundreds of dollars? Is this the evil of Capitalism or consumerism? Why is being free to buy or consume what you want bad and who gets to decide what is bad?

I also hear Capitalism is bad because it hurts workers. I did mention above how it creates jobs but let me hit on one other critique of Capitalism. I will admit in my previous example, the streamlining I mentioned does sometimes mean streamlining the production of the product which leads to the elimination of jobs. This is not a fault of Capitalism. It is part of it which is not understood and is thought of as unfair, especially when it is your job which is cut. When that job is cut however, it frees up more capital which can then be used for the aforementioned reasons or to create an entirely new product. The new product will require new and different skills to produce it. A new factory may be needed to manufacture the product and a new sales force must be created to market the product. This is what is known as the *creative destruction* part of Capitalism. It is not evil but necessary for companies and our country to grow and support a growing population.

It does however present a problem for those who resist the changing job requirements needed to grow in a capitalistic society. This is the problem I see as inherent in the company and union relationship. The companies need a work force that can change with the needs of the company to compete and thrive. Unions it seems to me are determined to resist transitions and want to focus on maintaining current positions and status. Catering to a competing interest within your organization is not a productive use of resources.

Some seem to believe Capitalism exploits the poor through low wages for workers. This is not true and is used to attack the system shouting exploitation as the problem. If one understands the Capitalist system, it is understood that wages for labor should be set by the market where employers have a job and a wage for a job. The wage is determined by the cost to produce the product. If the wage is too high and the product cannot be sold at a price which allows the company to cover expenses and a reasonable profit, it will not or should not be produced at all. To do otherwise is a destruction of capital which eventually leads to a decline of our standard of living.

When a government mandated minimum wage is thrown into the mix, this in some cases eliminates the company's ability to produce the good and sell it at a reasonable price and thereby eliminating the need for an additional employee. This is why having a minimum wage or increasing the minimum wage can hurt business but it also hurts the worker more by possibly eliminating his very job completely. Instead of earning a market wage agreed to by him and the company, *he receives no wages at all* due to the government mandated minimum wage. This then leads to the person with no job available to then fall back on government assistance which will basically pay him less than he would have received at the job the government had a direct hand in eliminating due to the minimum wage. Instead of his money coming from the company where his work is needed, his money comes from the U.S. Citizens at the so called benevolence of the federal government. What sense does this make? Now tell me, is this the evil of Capitalism? No, it is the evil of government intervention in private affairs.

Just to mention one more thing regarding government intervention into business, we cannot forget about the corporate tax. This tax is levied on business profits which again takes potential *capital* away from business preventing its use for capitalistic purposes in lieu of governmental and state purposes and programs. It handicaps Capitalism. The corporate tax is a punishing tax not on the corporations but on the people and the U.S. economy. A higher corporate tax on businesses means the business has to keep prices higher than necessary to pay the taxes and stay in business. So where does the company get the money to pay taxes? They get it from us, the people. We buy products at inflated prices with our money left over after federal withholding is deducted from our paychecks. Corporations pay taxes with the money they get from our purchase of their product or service. So who does it sound like to you that really pays taxes in this country? You and me, that's who. Corporations do not pay taxes; they in essence collect additional taxes from us, the citizens, and pass it on to the government. This is nothing more than double taxation of the people.

Profits or capital is the fuel for the engine of Capitalism. If the fuel is taken away or reduced, which is what the corporate tax does, it directly hinders the capitalist system. It kills jobs and hurts the livelihoods of citizens. The engine will not run without fuel, i.e. the capital that comes from profits or investments by people.

Finally, one last thing which needs to be said about the corporate tax and how it and the minimum wage are a danger to the United States economy and jobs: These two government mandates on business are two of the prime reasons companies outsource their jobs to foreign countries. They are two of the reasons why America does not have a manufacturing base any longer. These additional costs placed on business by politicians keep prices high and take jobs from Americans by forcing business to find ways to stay operating and competitive. My question is when companies are looked at as un-American because they take their jobs overseas, why are these factors so easily brushed aside? Why is blame not placed on the political policy and those who support it which causes the company's action instead of the desperate action by the company to merely try to stay in business? This is attacking a symptom, not a cause and is an easy tactic used by politicians to attack business, big or small. Seems to be a reasonable thing to ponder when we are talking about the evils of Capitalism, doesn't it?

What is the role of the average U.S. Citizen in Capitalism? We the People can also be a source of needed capital in our free capitalistic system by investing our saving for a reasonable rate of return. We have just gone through a time in U.S. history where the saving rate was negative. This meant we spent more than we made. This is not good for governments, not good for us, and not good for an economy based on capitalism. When we save part of our income instead of spending it we will encourage the economy to prosper based on *saving* instead of spending. When we spend, we do create more demand for products and services but many times this is done through the use of carrying excessive debt. So not only did we spend everything we made but we have to pay interest on the debt as well. Good for bankers, go figure, but not for us or our nation.

The better and more sound way to encourage economic activity is through saving more. It may be slower but I believe we will be better off in the long run. When we invest our excess dollars by either putting it in a saving account, or buying a CD or bond, we are allowing others, both individuals and companies to utilize *our* capital in exchange for a return on our money. We can choose high risk or low for our money. Then our capital is used in the economy to again create new products and operations, open new plants or facilities, build more schools, etc. It is a wonderful thing if we would just allow it to happen and get government out of our way. These actions all create more jobs and more *permanent* jobs while increasing our standard of living through the use of available capital, i.e. money. Now I ask again, is this the evil of Capitalism?

I often hear or read regarding Capitalism that there are those who get rich off an unsuspecting public due to companies or people cheating in the Capitalist system. This may be true in a small number of cases but in the big picture it is not. There will always be cheaters, there always have and always will be. Nothing can prevent someone from trying to get something for free and cheat or scam others to do it. When caught, those companies or people such as Bernie Madoff should be hammered without mercy accordingly based on their crimes.

Some say Capitalism favors the rich and only the rich get richer and the poor get poorer. I disagree completely. I think Capitalism favors the exceptional, the do-er. It favors those with the drive to succeed and produce things others want. I will admit, for those who remain fence sitters and refuse to better themselves through education, working harder, being more productive and always trying to make things better, a capitalistic system will be difficult for them. The capitalist system is fitting for an ambitious and self-reliant society. It rewards those who use exceptional traits. Does Capitalism favor the rich? No, it favors the innovative and those who can move forward despite the odds. Those who can as Norman Schwarzkopf said at a lecture I attended, "When in charge, Take charge." This quote has really stuck with me over the years. If you are this type of person I believe you are likely to become as rich as you desire to be. Now rich is a subjective term depending on the individual and their definition of rich. To me, rich means earning enough money to have a decent home, take care of my family, and have some fun now and then. That's it for me. Is that selfish? Do I not have the right to pursue happiness in this fashion without someone else deciding what is best for me or whether my definition of rich is unfair to them or someone else?

Capitalism forces you to take chances and continuously improve; you cannot get comfortable for too long, else you fail. Perhaps this is why so many dislike the capitalist system. Capitalism is based on results instead of good intentions. You can have all the good intentions in the world but a good intention has never accomplished a single thing without a decision and the drive to take action and see what happens knowing the potential for consequences or mistakes. I have heard people say successful people are just lucky. That is probably true on rare occasions but I think it to be the exception rather than the rule. I see this kind of statement as a way for fence sitters to attempt to discredit all the work it took for the successful person to get where they are. It is a way to allow the fence sitter to simply stay where they are, in permanent stagnation.

I'm a great believer in luck, and I find the harder I work the more I have of it
-Thomas Jefferson

This U.S. Citizen

Chapter 15: The American Way

A problem lies in there will always exist an inability or unwillingness of many citizens and immigrants to understand, practice, and pass on the ideals and values which make America great while at the same time expecting to benefit forever from these ideals. If the values and ideals are not continued, the greatness they expect to enjoy is dead. To use a car engine metaphor again, if you ride in a car but do not believe or understand the concept a car needs an engine in order to move, you will not go anywhere no matter how much you hope. By not continuing the ideals inherent in the founding of the United States of America, we are allowing sugar to be poured in our gas tank of ideals and then wondering why there is no movement!

What sense does it make to incorporate the cultures, customs, and beliefs of the rest of the world into our nation and expect it to continue to prosper? People came to America *because* it was different from the rest of the world. These differences are the American Way! These differences are what make the United States great and what has created the most free and successful society to have ever existed in the history of human beings. The United States of America is not great despite these ideals, but because of them and today these American ideals are considered second rate values when compared to those of the rest of the world. The American Way *is* the culture of the United States and is a more important culture to preserve than any other to have existed in the past. Many people just do not realize it because they have always benefited and have been immersed in it. They simply cannot conceive or imagine it disappearing.

This belief allows them to ignore signs of decline or reversion to ways not conducive to success in America. They have never tasted personally real hardship as is known in other parts of the world or in the past. People leave other terrible parts of the world and come here for a reason. They come here for the freedom to do what they want and to be left alone. Why then do we allow the politically correct accommodation of un-American cultures and beliefs to permeate and place The American Way on the back burner?

In order for the United States of America to survive with its original ideals we must all face one fact: Just showing up is not enough! We as citizens must make a focused and deliberate effort to take care of this country and not *hope* someone else will do it. We are that someone. If we all rely on someone else to pull our weight because we have other things to do, we will continue on the path to the inevitable decay of the fabric of The American Way. Doesn't anyone remember nor have respect for Truth, Justice, and The American Way? In the last Superman movie which came out a few years ago *The American Way* was conveniently left out of what Superman fights for. I took this as a direct insult from Hollywood and cannot consider forgiveness for this attempt to damage an image of American culture.

We citizens must stop putting *our nation* at the bottom of our to-do list to get to later but instead make it a conscious and daily cause of preserving The American Way. If American exceptionalism decays we will not have to worry much about those other things on our list because none of it will matter. All will have been destroyed or confiscated for the greater good or to spread around so everyone can have a portion even when they did not earn it. All in the name of fairness when no one ever asks or answers the question: Fairness according to whom?

The bottom line is human nature makes us complacent. We are all guilty in some way shape or form. What we have to do differently from now on is realize when we are complacent and put a stop to it. We must forever instill conscious of complacency and be more aware when we must take action and cross an ocean from time to time to renew The American Way and forever protect it.

I mentioned before some people just do not realize how good they have here in the United States. They do not know or understand just how lucky they are to be in the freest country in the world. America is not free from problems or perfect but I would not trade my citizenship for anything. I hear people asking what is going on in this country or what is happening to America when they talk about certain issues. Well I thought about it and the way I solve problems is first I consciously think whether the negative issue at hand is simply a symptom or is it indeed the underlying cause. If it is a symptom, I move on. Part of the problem today is based on the fact people or politicians try too hard to merely remedy symptoms instead of finding the cause behind the symptom. People focus on symptoms because there usually can be a quick fix which will make things better long enough to forget the issue. I also believe this to be one of the major faults in government today. A quick fix can easily be touted at election time as a good decision but is only discovered later, the problem still persists. The politician has to hope we the people forget by the next election year. Sad thing is, we usually do. Don't we?

We allow politicians to fix symptoms because to address a real cause would be too hard for them *and for us* and would most likely require a transition taking us out of our comfort zone, maybe permanently. How scary, for any politician! If our politicians do not have the character and the courage to address and solve big issues because they fear the fallout, then we need new politicians. It is that simple. We need people who will solve problems today before they escalate over time into issues which can permanently damage our nation, freedoms, and The American Way. Better to climb a small hill now than have to conquer a mountain down the road is a strategy I would gladly follow.

The Pursuit of Happiness

Part of our problem today is how some individuals and politicians choose to interpret the words of the Constitution and the Declaration of Independence. How is it right a nation's government created by a Declaration of Independence today works to create and support policies that create *dependence* of its people on their government?

The areas which come to mind are the inalienable Rights of Life, Liberty, and the Pursuit of Happiness. I want to specifically address the latter of the three. Since this book is based on my thoughts and concerns I would to share the meaning of the Pursuit of Happiness as I understand. You may of course disagree. To put it simply, I do not believe the Pursuit of Happiness in American society and as written in the Declaration of Independence in anyway, shape, or form provides a *guarantee* of happiness. To place blame on society or that there are major flaws in our free capitalistic society because some people are not as happy as they wish they were is appalling to me.

Our founding documents were created to lay out a foundation where people could be free to create their own destiny and path for success. If some people choose not to create a destiny, whose fault is that? Mine? Yours? If given basic laws to abide by versus stifling over regulation and control, people will thrive. Correction, people with drive, determination, and who hold themselves responsible as the determining factor will thrive. Those who do not possess these attributes will have difficulty until they gain them. These are not traits or talents which cannot be learned but are attributes we as U.S. Citizens should incorporate in everything we do. This is the American spirit we need to preserve. To preserve the right to go after an opportunity when it arises and create more opportunity is the role of a good government, not to guarantee an outcome and a result of our action based on *any* definition of fairness.

Fairness

I often hear how the United States is fundamentally an unfair system where some people are not rewarded with the same pay as some others, all things being equal. I support the often used phrase equal work for equal pay but the emphasis must be placed on the words *equal work* instead of equal pay. Equal work to me means equal effort and results. I firmly believe if one gives equal effort and gets equal results, they will be paid the same as another person who does the same in most cases. There are and will always be exceptions. If America becomes a place where rewards on pay do not directly relate to effort and results, the American society and system will falter. How can we have a discussion regarding fairness of pay for equal work without bringing up the issue that *all people do not give equal effort and do not get equal results?*

Two people who show up for the same job are likely to do the job slightly different or even drastically different. One will eventually be rewarded more if the way they do the job is in line with how their boss believes it should be done. That person is more likely to get a raise or promotion in a well run organization, while the person not doing things according to instruction from management will not. Unless we are our own boss and even then, our boss is our customer, we will always have someone we do work for. Our job is simply to do what it takes to make the boss or customer happy with our daily work and we will be rewarded. Sometimes we are rewarded in the time frame and how we expect, sometimes not. Either way we are free to seek other options. If you are constantly working at an organization where you know absolutely you are doing your best but still can not compete with others around you, *you* must do something about it.

The something you need to do is find out why you have a short fall or why others do better than you. You only have the ability to change yourself and what you do. It is unlikely an attempt to change others to see things your way will work, especially if they are more successful than you. A good place to start is to simply ask them for advice. People like to help others and some people will help you. Some may not but you should be okay with that as well. If at the end of this discovery process you find you still cannot perform at the needed level or level you desire, perhaps it is now time to seek other options as freedom allows you to do. Chances are this will get you closer to discovering your real talents at another job or after re-tooling your mind or skill set.

You will be treated more fairly because you will have learned new abilities and earned your rewards. Either way, you are then more likely to be able to give the effort and results needed at the job and will enjoy your pursuit of happiness more as well.

Accountability

The lack of accountability is something I believe has permeated in the last twenty to thirty years with the aging of the baby boomers to the sixties free love generation up to Generation X and finally Generation Y. I once went to a seminar about working with Generation Y people which was focused on to how to keep Gen Y'ers happy in the workplace. The suggestions were shocking. It might as well have been about how to keep five year olds happy. The main theme was to make sure they are not bored and constantly tell them how great they are even to the point of suggesting employers call their parents to tell them how great they are. In my mind I was thinking, what about the paycheck they get? Is that not good enough anymore?

I once had a boss tell me after my attempt at holding an employee accountable for their work and time out of the office I had a *take no prisoners* attitude. He told me it was my fault for not communicating better with the employee. Does take no prisoners mean as their supervisor I cannot simply tell them to do something the way it needs to be done? Every time I gave them something to do they would say they were *"busy"*, or would *"try to get to it"* or would *"try to remember"* etc, etc. They always would simply not listen to how it needed to be done and would do it their own way. Now please don't think me a tyrant but in some cases things need to be done in a specific way for specific reasons and other times they do not and it does not matter how it gets done. The problem was this person *always* would do things their way and take offense when something was said. This was followed several times by loud outbursts in the office caused by nothing more than attempting to have some accountability for actions taken by this employee. At this point the boss became involved and excuses were made for this employee by the boss. At this point I asked my boss this question: So we have to give our people a paycheck for working here, give them work to do, and also kiss their ass to get them to do it as well? His answer was yes. My jaw was on the floor and probably a good thing the discussion was taking place by phone. I said he was going to have to show me how to do that because I was probably going to find great difficulty in completing such a task. Turned out, this person was laid off eventually for completely different reasons so I guess the problem solved itself.

If this is kind of mentality does exist in the real business world, and I know now that it does, it is not good for America. This is not the kind of work ethic and accountability that will preserve American principles and ideals to keep America great. It should not be tolerated.

A point I would like to make is that when times are good, this lack of accountability can permeate and is more tolerated but when times get tough, these people will almost always be the first to go. If they were very reliable and valuable to the business in the first place, their likelihood of being let go would be less. In a downturn, a business will keep its most valuable people and ride out the storm. You can always staff back up for the low skill jobs at anytime. So in my opinion, when people are not held accountable, you are not helping them, you are actually hurting them because you prevent them from improving their skills and abilities in ways which will make them indispensable. Such is the potential evil of welfare, in whatever form it may come.

Central Planning and Freedom do not mix

If everyone knew the outcome or result of every action they took or that it could be *planned*, the value would be diminished in taking the risk. For example, if it was guaranteed getting a college degree meant you would absolutely get a job making $50,000 per year; wouldn't everyone get a college degree? So getting a college degree now equals a $50,000 job. Now if everyone had a degree and a 50k year job, what would be the factor which determined the annual pay for those wanting to make more than 50k? A particular school, field of study, grade point average, etc. would also have to be determined and a pay scale associated with it. Who decides the scale? Who decides what fair pay at each level is and based on what criteria? My point is when you guarantee a result you must also *control* every affecting factor associated with the guarantee and there in lies the problem.

This leads to the notion governments can predict and control all of these factors and is the downfall of the central planning theory and model many in government try to follow today. For central planning to work you must do something which goes absolutely against the tenets of the founding documents and freedom of the individual. You must control everything individuals do and how they live. This is not freedom and not the American Way. It must be brought to light every time it is attempted and thus thwarted. To consider and use individuals as merely small cogs in a large societal plan is to diminish the individuals' right to life, liberty, and their definition of happiness. In a planned society, someone or group is creating the plan. My question is what if I as a citizen of the United States do not like the plan? Do I not matter anymore in deciding what happens to me since I am no longer included in the discussions of how I am to be governed? I am starting to wonder, are you?

World Approval, why do we need it?

It is simply now time to get back to basics in our country including hard work, high expectations, high accountability, and the freedom to pursue happiness in the fashion we as individual U.S. citizens decide for

159

ourselves. We must focus on these American ideals first and stop looking for world approval in everything we do as a nation. If we care too much about world approval we will take on the characteristics they approve of which leads us away from those aspects of America and its founding principles which makes the United States great.

The reason people left Europe and other parts of the world to come to the United States of America is because they did not want to live in those places anymore and wanted the ideals of freedom the United States offered. What sense does it make to do away with those ideals? Is it not what we are doing by looking to the rest of the world for their approval and consensus on how to govern our country?

Please indulge me with yet one more example to make a point. A physically battered and mentally abused woman, lets call her Betsy, after years of abuse and restriction by an over controlling spouse, lets call him George, decides to leave the abusive relationship. By staying with George, Betsy knew she could never live her life the way she wanted or believed was best for her. Once free of the control of the abuser, George, she then moves to another part of the country. Having been free now for years, she has been able to become a stronger and self reliant person who is able to meet new people as well as meeting a new spouse who is very good to her. She also gets educated because there are more schools and opportunities to learn available to her. Betsy also now has a new family of beautiful children and her life is good. She also manages to have a long and fruitful career for herself allowing her to save money for her retirement and enough to send her kids to very good schools as well. Now things are going very well for Betsy but by some illogical reasoning she now *feels* it would the right thing to do to get George's opinion about how she is living her life. She feels it is now important George approve of her daily actions and without this approval, she will never be a true success. It is at this point where George and his ideas are invited back by Betsy and she starts incorporating his ideas back into her life decisions. This includes George's way of raising her children, managing her money, where she should live, and deciding what schools her children should attend.

So after reading this short and sad story I would ask what good reason was there for inviting a former abuser and his ideas back into Betsy's life when there was so much proof she was better off without his ideas or approval? Did she feel bad for George? Did she have a need for him to like her no matter how bad his policies or ideas were? Did she not want him to feel rejected and feel bad because she had been so successful? Did Betsy feel guilty she was now more successful than George?

Betsy should have left George back in his *old world* and she should have stayed in the new world she had *created for herself.* She was doing just fine without George's opinion was she not? So, shall the United States be better off when we once again have the clear mindset we will do what is best for our country, our sovereignty, and our people and not make decisions based on the approval of the rest of the world? Simply because we put the interest of our country first does not mean it is to the detriment of our neighboring countries around the world but again, if we must always wait on consensus for everyone to agree, nothing will ever get done.

The United States will again be the inspiration by example which leads others to mirror *some* of our ideals. In that action, they will also benefit from the use of those ideals.

Chapter 16: Bias?

Paying attention

To most U.S. Citizens, politics is too slow and boring to stay involved because it takes sometimes long periods of time to accomplish things. Unfortunately our attention deficit in this area has come to haunt us in that a government which is not overseen by its people will take advantage of them and their complacency by enriching themselves and increasing their power. We must again force ourselves to make the difficult choice and choose the uphill battle to get back control of our runaway government to the point where it again understands its purpose is to work *for us* instead of their self perceived purpose of doing what they think *is best for us.*

The difference in these two purposes is drastically different and we are now seeing what living under a system based on the latter feels like. The latter includes an obvious assumption of intellectual superiority on their part and I do not know about you but this citizen does not like it. I am starting to feel more and more like being boxed in or herded into doing things and following so many government mandated regulations and guidelines it is beginning to affect me. I am feeling less like a free citizen of my country and more like a controlled *subject* whose purpose is to produce and consume for the good of the federal government and *its* needs and goals. Our government should not have needs and goals other than providing for security against our enemies, and helping its citizens increase their freedom and standard of living.

What is going on now is not the American Way. This may be an agreeable way to govern in other countries around the world but not here in the United States. This is the destination where people go when they do not want to live under that type of system. We have to stop this from happening here because we unfortunately have no sanctuary of sanity to run to. We must stop touting term limits and start making government oversight a citizen participating endeavor instead of a spectator sport!

An AmericanThinker.com commenter initials CEW wrote on Feb. 18, 2010, "Reminds me of a number of friends of mine who have said they have no interest in politics. I would normally remind them that this is foolish – since politics most certainly has an interest in them." Truer words have never been spoken in my opinion. Thank you CEW.

Polling and the News

We now live in a world of continuous news and continuous polling. This continuous polling is supposed to help everyone understand what others think about an issue but I think these polls are too numerous and in many cases biased from the get go. Many are biased in the questions they ask by loading a question for example: *How bad to you think _____ is for America?* This type of question has built in a premise assuming

_____ is bad and the pollster is just trying to see how bad people think it really is. Then to make it worse, the poll is done using only readers of a certain newspaper whose reader base is already biased to the paper's political slant. So a slanted question is polled to a slanted base of responders and the results are treated as kosher? If it favors a politician's cause it is used time and time again and I never hear anyone mention a concern regarding the accuracy of the poll, as long as the margin of error is shown. This kind of poll looks credible and is used to persuade the uninformed. The only way to fight this is to become informed so when you see this kind of polling, an automatic light goes off in your head making you think who, what, and most important – why was this poll done. Why was this poll done and who will benefit from the conclusions it makes? Fact is, polls are done for a reason and I think when the reason is to persuade instead of inform we must be on the lookout. Lastly when a poll is used as evidence against a politician's cause, the politician will usually just say they do not believe the poll anyway.

News, does it exist anymore? People report the news with a bias based on their ideological beliefs. That is all there is to it nowadays in my opinion. Tom Brokaw said once that journalists will always be needed to interpret information for the public. Inherent in his statement is an elitist assumption of superiority and it should insult anyone who hears it. It is a nice way to say you are too stupid to understand the news on your own. The problem is Tom, your interpretation if I wanted it from you would be biased to your beliefs and ideology. There is no way around it.

More journalists are simply liberal thinkers, artsy, and creative right brained people. It is what they do. It is what they are! Their talent is geared to story telling and I think a lot of times reporting what happened gets mixed up in a creative person's *need* to tell a story and gain recognition. People are going to write a story they find interesting and a story they believe in. I don't think they will expend much time, energy, and creative talent trying to make sure they show a side of a story *which goes against and diminishes their personal opinions.* For example, do you or I spend a lot of time doing things we do not like to do? A logical conclusion would be a journalist probably does not either, would it not? It would be like trying to use your right hand to write if you are a left handed person, no pun intended. You just cannot do it. Well, very few can and I think this applies to news and broadcast journalists as well. They simply gravitate to other people and organizations who think like they do.

I simply believe based on my experience with understanding people that more right brain creative type people go to journalism school and attend liberal arts oriented universities. More left brain analytical, reason focused people go into science, business, finance, etc. Not all but most. So everyone talks about how the media is biased and I think it is true but to understand why might be just as important to understand.

These right brained creative people are not the kind of people who are content or feel good about themselves or their work if they were to only *report* the news. Reporting to them would be simply listing or showing the events which unfolded during the day and would be a rather boring endeavor for creative minded people. I feel today a journalist wants their work to be influential and have tremendous meaning but if that journalist is biased politically, to what cause will the story look to benefit? If a story pushes right or left, democrat or republican, liberal or conservative, is this really *reporting* the news or just another *interpretation* of the news? Both sides of the media are indeed guilty of this and I do not believe there is any way around it save one.

Each individual person must have the ability to decipher the news as reported to them and stop complaining about the media bias because it will never change or go away. It is not *media* bias; it is *personal, individual* bias. They are who they are just like we are who we are. To become an informed and educated citizen, ready to defend the Constitution and the rights it preserves, there is only one way. It is a long and sometimes difficult process but a necessary one. The difficult task is to learn the skill of reading and I am not simply talking about the act of reading. I am talking about reading with the ability to filter difficult and sometimes confusing material. The material should be American history, world history, biographies, economics, capitalism, socialism, communism, fascism, textbooks, business books, finance books, economics, and politics of course. Anything and everything you can. Reading this material gets easier over time and you will start honing in on the subject which interests you most. From there you will love reading because when you finally get to a point where you realize how much information there is out there, you will hunger for more. The best thing I have ever learned is that I now know how much I still do not know and it bothers me.

The key to being able to become your own filter for what is put out as news daily is to become informed and well read. The point to strive for when absorbing the news today is to not only focus or concentrate merely on *what* is being reported. You must also be consciously aware of *how* the news is being reported. Once this skill is attained, paying attention to what is going on in the United States and in the world takes on a whole new meaning. If we turn our attention to discover what exactly the journalist is trying to convince us into believing, we can only then make our *own* conclusions. This way we are not subject to the news event which took place wrapped tightly in the journalists' assumptions and opinion of how we should think about it. When we have the skill and knowledge to make our own *individual* conclusions, we will truly have reinvigorated and are ready to carry on the American spirit.

Chapter 17:   Enemy of the U.S.

This Marine's thoughts on war, military, and our enemy.

It is time we accept the fact there are foreign enemies of the United States of America who are highly determined and able to harm the American system and kill U.S. citizens. We must do what it takes to stop them.

The war in Afghanistan is now in its 8th year as I am writing, already lasting twice as long as WWII when we helped defeat the Italian, German, and the Japanese empires. Why is it taking so long to end our involvement in Afghanistan? I am a Marine but not a war fighting expert and I have not been in combat but I call things as I see them. The mission is flawed in my opinion. I saw a Frontline special in October, 2009 showing what was happening on the ground in June, 2009 in Helmand province. I was amazed and shocked the 20 year old Marine's mission had morphed into trying to convince locals they were there to help them. The Marine was also asking them to help defeat the Taliban and convince them it was safe in the area. The locals said "you have tanks, guns, helicopters, etc. and we do not even have a sword so what can we do?"

I thought this to be profound not only in the response but in the entire situation regarding placing that kind of responsibility on a 20 year old Marine. He is not a diplomat. He is a rifleman, sworn and trained to protect the United States and the Constitution by killing the enemy. Diplomacy is for the diplomats. The people in Afghanistan have been living their tribal ways for a thousand years and they are not going to change simply because we are there. They are not going to respect and follow a centralized government they never see in a far away capital city. They just do not think that way and will not anytime soon. Does this justify a permanent presence there until they get with our idea of how to live their lives? I don't think so. These Afghans are being told how to live their lives by an out of touch Afghan government and a foreign military presence which keeps them in a permanent state of nervousness. They probably feel much like we U.S. Citizens today being told how we should live our lives by our government. Our government that tells us what kind of car we should be driving, how our healthcare should be managed, what kind and how much energy we should use, what kind of food we should eat and on and on. We do not like it and I do not think the Afghans do either. I think it is time to leave them alone to figure out how to run their own country and start worrying about our own again.

Now on the other side, I need to speak as a former member of the military and give my opinion of what this citizen believes should have happened in Afghanistan. First of all Afghanistan is a country which harbored terrorists and terrorist groups that unleashed and succeeded in a plot which killed 3,000 people on American soil. They caused billions in dollars damage to our economy. They attacked the head of our military, the Pentagon. They attacked our financial center and *destroyed forever* an American *icon*; the Twin Towers of the World Trade Center and an icon which stood in one of our nation's and one of the world's greatest cities; New York City. This was the largest and costliest attack to ever have been executed against the United States of America. This was an act of war and should be treated as such. This justified going after them. We should have gone into Afghanistan and killed them. That should have been and should now be the only mission. Quick, hard, and fast should have been the tactic to fight this war. Nation building, trust of the locals, stable government; these things are good long term goals but they should be the internal goals of the Afghans, not ours.

If the Afghans are not ready to change to a democratic system, they will not just because we think it best for them. Hunting down and killing the enemy is the goal. It is simple, straightforward and most of all it is a mission those in the military are ready to execute on a moments notice and give their lives for. *It is this U.S. Citizen's opinion that it is not worth the life of a single Marine or any soldier to see to it a mud hut street market is open so locals can trade vegetables.* Is that a goal really worth risking a serviceman's life to achieve? Does the fact we go into a country who harbors the enemy or terrorist in order to kill them mean we owe said country a Marshall Plan to take them from the Stone Age to the Modern Age? I'm sorry but NO!

We, the United States should focus directly on killing the enemy. War is hell and people die especially when they bring it upon themselves. Innocents will die when they are in close proximity to our enemy and is a reason why wars should end as soon as possible. Sometimes innocent people die but that is part of the price you pay in war when you attack the United States or any other free society. We may not get them the entire enemy but we will get many of them. Then we leave and go home, mission accomplished and to hell with what others say about it. As time goes by we monitor the area and we keep people there on the ground and in the area learning, watching, and listening for the enemy and when we see the enemy rise again or reform, we attack again and kill them. We let them know constantly we will be back on a moments notice if we see them again. This mission is an offensive mission instead of the defensive mission of staying too long and becoming a permanent target. Some think once we take an area and clean it of the enemy we must hold it. Why? To prevent them from taking it back? So what, let them come back. At least we know where they are then and then we attack them again and kill even more of them. Am I getting my point across here? Eventually they will get the idea the United States means business and it probably is risky to one's life if they continue in their ways. It gives them the choice: keep fighting and die, or stop and live a life. Either choice means it ends quickly which is good for America.

War should not be a choice based on party politics. If attacked we have the right and duty to end the attack and stop it from happening again. Another thing that seems to have arisen lately is the notion of a measured response. To my understanding this is retaliation only using similar force which was used against you. What sense does this stupidity make? How is this expected to end a situation? Also just this week in Feb. 2010 rules of engagement have changed for our soldiers in that they cannot return fire unless they can actually *see* a weapon. What do politicians think just whizzed by a Serviceman's head making that distinctive crack as a round goes by, a spitball? Again this is a moronic way to fight a war. This is not fighting a war; this is trying to manage a war and its political problems. If you doubt me, read Sun Tzu.

If someone has a knife and you have a gun, you do not put your gun away thereby risking losing a knife fight and your life do you? No, you tell the other party to put down the knife and if they do not and they come at you, you take action *with the gun* putting an end to the threat, permanently.

So my war fighting and military philosophy is pretty straightforward in having a strong, ready military to take care of threats quickly and come home. That's it. That is the Wernecke Doctrine on war. Is this not a reasonable policy which will end the enemy threat as quickly as possible and risk as few American lives and innocents as possible? If the rest of the world knows this to be our policy will it not deter those who want to harm us?

Regarding the *rights* of the enemy.

Finally let me make on additional point regarding giving constitutional rights to the enemy. I am specifically referring to not only the Gitmo prisoners who may be tried in U.S. courts but the most recent enemy terrorist captured on Christmas day, 2009. This person is a Nigerian. He is not a United States Citizen. Rights of United States Citizens are just that. He is the enemy, NOT a common criminal. What he did was to attempt to commit an act of war against the United States of America and it citizenry. Those who give this enemy the rights of U.S. citizens and a trial by a jury of his peers are absolute fools as to the understanding of our country, our customs, our culture, our Constitution and our right to eliminate those who threaten our existence. This enemy attempted to destroy the property of and slaughter citizens of the United States for fanatical and ideological reasoning.

Although his plot failed, it was a failure on his part due to blind luck. His act was equivalent to lining up 300 U.S. citizens including men, women, and children during wartime, putting a pistol to each of their foreheads and pulling the trigger with the *intended expectation* he was about to blow their brain through the back of their head. The only thing which stopped it was a misfire. Sorry about the graphic description of my example but what is the difference in this and plunging 300 people which could have been you or me or any of our family members in a crashing fireball, probably killing even

174

more victims on the ground? These people are our enemy and should be treated as the Germans were in WWII when they attempted to enter the United States as saboteurs. They were found guilty by military tribunal and six went to the electric chair. I would have preferred firing squad. One was given hard labor for life and another was given thirty years in prison. At least FDR did the right thing in this instance. This Nigerian should be interrogated for information, then given a military tribunal and hopefully found guilty and sentenced to death by the aforementioned firing squad. DONE! No prison, no Gitmo, dead. Now that is a deterrent.

History does not long entrust the care of freedom to the weak or the timid.
-Dwight D. Eisenhower

This U.S. Citizen

Chapter 18:   The Duty of the Citizen

What do we do? How do we take back control of our government and protect the ideals which made the United States of America that shining city on the hill Ronald Reagan described?

We need to do many things. We need to re-educate ourselves as to how *different* a society based on individual freedom is from societies that are not. We need to pass down ethics and morals inherent in the founding of our nation. A focus on fairness is not an American ideal. Equality of opportunity is the goal, not equality of results. We need to create a standard of what is expected of every United States Citizen. We need to use the time provided by our freedom and success to better ourselves and our minds. American exceptionalism has provided us with leisure time to do great things because of the efficiency created by talented and exceptional people. It would be shameful to waste the gift of freedom we possess. Let us not continue to waste this gift we have as Americans but let us fight everyday against the natural decay which comes with being comfortable.

Put simply, we need to make better choices, choose carefully, and always think about the possible outcomes. We need to choose the hard things in life. One of the most memorable quotes I know is from John F. Kennedy when he said: "We choose to go to the moon and do the other things not because they are easy but because they are hard." We went to the moon but we can always work better and harder at the other things in life. Difficulty and struggle builds character and self esteem. Our free society allows people to go through their lives if they choose always making the easy choices. I think sometime unconsciously because they are comfortable and/or afraid of failure. It is my opinion that someone who remains a fence sitter, one who always makes the easy decisions will not amount to much of anything in their lives and it makes me sad to see such opportunity squandered when I see it. This is the human nature aspect we must become aware of and internally as a nation of citizens, struggle to overcome. We must be conscious of our decisions and ask ourselves *why am I making this choice? Is it best for me and my country in the long run or am I looking for a quick fix? Where will it likely lead?*

When we choose the easy route we learn nothing and we gain very little. It is when the difficult choice is made which requires long periods of effort, focus, struggle, thought, and many times risk of failure that results in something worthwhile in life. Risk and hard fought effort is what builds a person of good character and confidence. This is American Spirit. You know people like this. Most likely you look up to them because you want to be like them in some ways. You can and I can. It only takes the willingness to do the hard things in life and be willing to put in your time. Few things worth having or of real meaningful value in life come easy. If they did, everyone would have them. This could be either material things or personal attributes that people of strong character possess. You can only legally possess these things by earning them in an honest way or learning for yourself, in a way that required hard fought internal drive and effort.

We must fight human nature and the urge to make the easy choice or the choice which allows us to stay in our comfort zone. To keep America great it is our duty to do this. We must educate our children to think about this starting as young as possible. Help our children understand risk taking and how it helps grow us as individuals. We must also teach consequences and understand them. To take risk is to understand the consequences and willingly accept them if and when they come. Sometimes we fail but if we think through the possible outcomes, we will most likely not be overwhelmed if things go array and they will. But this is not bad, this is America. We learn the most from the mistakes we make in life. Taking risks and making mistakes gives us more information which allows us to make better decisions in the future. It opens doors, gives us new routes and other choices to make. A person who never takes risks or makes decisions will never see new choices or opportunities. They remain not knowing what they do not know. They stay comfortable in their state of not knowing very much at all. This is not an American ideal.

> *Do not fear mistakes. You will know failure.*
> *Continue to reach out.*
> -Benjamin Franklin

*Someone who fears failure will never really know
the true taste of success. For to achieve success one
must risk failure.*
-James D Wernecke

Think about what kind of person you are and be honest with yourself. If you think you are weak at something, admit it. If you do, the next time you have to make a decision you will be more aware of your weakness in the past and may be more likely to make a different decision. Do not beat yourself up if your fail at first. Knowing why you failed now gives you the tools to do better and try again. You still may fail but you may just learn that one small piece of information which was missing before and it is now enough to lead to success. This is American Spirit. Make your goals smaller and more easily achievable. Do not take on more than you can handle but do push yourself to try to do more than you think you can. If you break things up into sections to conquer one at a time you achieve something big by succeeding a little at a time. Life is a slow process and most of the time, success is as well. Success, like life is a journey. You have to enjoy the journey and smell the roses instead of worrying about getting to the end of the road. Over time you will become more of a do-er like America's founders and ready to pass on that American Spirit instead of the fence sitter who decided maybe I'll cross that ocean tomorrow but never does.

Now if you are a do-er and you know who you are. It is your obligation to pass on the American Spirit to others, especially to those who lack it. The feeling of being part of something bigger than yourself and making a contribution to the preservation of the United States of America as the founders created it is worth the continued effort. Take notice of those who do not possess the drive and spirit you possess and talk to them. It will be hard at first. Some will be open to ideals they are not accustomed to hearing and will need additional motivation. Some people will not care no matter what and those people; you must leave behind because they may unfortunately be a lost cause in the preservation of our founding principles. I am realistic and I know there will always be those who cannot be helped so we must focus on those who can benefit from your spirit of taking action and making a difference. It is our duty and our debt to the Founding Fathers who pledged their lives and their fortunes to create a new way of life for us. To honor those who died for our freedom on foreign shores, we owe it to them as well. I know I do.

I have talked about what I believe to be influencing the decay of American ideals and how we can overcome them. We are possibly reverting to the mindset of the rest of the world due to fear of passing judgment, fear of upsetting or offending someone, and the lack of accountability by people and parents to the ideals which founded the United States of America. This means we have failed at the task of conserving those ideals and passing them on for the specific purpose of preserving the American Way, the American system, and the American way of life. The term conservatism specifically is the belief in preserving and protecting these ideals and founding principles and comes directly from the definition of conserve which is to preserve, save, keep, protect, and safeguard. To safeguard the Constitution is the Rule; everything else should fall under this Rule. Lip service to an oath of office is not enough and we have ventured down a path where the Constitution is not the first consideration and thus we end up where we are today, approaching despotism. If collectivism was ever to be useful, a collectivist effort on the part of the U.S. citizenry to protect the Constitution from meddling politicians and their damaging agendas would be an acceptable use. This is the only instance where collectivism should be part of the United States of America.

This U.S. Citizen has spent now scores of pages explaining what he thinks about the causes and given some solutions to what is going on in our country. He would like to hear everyone reading this say the words and think *This U.S. Citizen* followed by what you believe and think. Do not be timid in speaking about our founding ideals. Write it in a book, on a website, say it to your neighbor, to your family members, to your co-workers, and especially to your children, on a sign, at a tea party and repeated to your representative and senators. If they do not listen, run against them or work with and support those who will for the sake of the United States of America.

Say the words This U.S. Citizen... and you decide what comes next in the quote and what comes next for our country. We are empowered by the Constitution to stand up to an oppressive federal government. It is time for the real power of this country to speak and finally be heard because we have been silent too long and we are now paying the price for our complacency. This U.S. Citizen not only wants to hear your words but the more important point is every other U.S. Citizen needs to hear what you think and believe. We all need to know we are not alone in our thoughts and that *our* ideals are still the ones which made America great and will allow it to remain that way. This U.S. Citizen does not want to be told what to do, what is best for him, and will not be tread upon any longer. We must come together as a group of individuals, as U.S. citizens, focused directly on the same object, to expound the greatness of America and the ideals which made it so. It is time for the next generation of American leaders to step up and take charge of protecting the freedoms of the U.S. Citizens. It is apparent our current group of leaders is not up to the task because they do not even understand the cause of Liberty. *They can no longer be trusted with such an important undertaking.*

The price of freedom is vigilance.
-Thomas Jefferson

So what happened in the elections of 2010 an 2012?

Elections were held and new representatives and senators were elected while others lost their seats for the straightforward reason that they were no longer trustworthy enough to fulfill their oath to the people and to the Constitution of the United States. The U.S. was taken to the brink of government meddling *with our very lives* and the people stood up and said no, not this. The do-ers showed up and took action, promising they would not be lulled back to sleep. They would closely monitor our representatives and participate in lawmaking and the operations of our officials who are so dutifully entrusted with the care of our precious republic. The people have vowed to support only those candidates who will correct the problems created by the latest political agenda and by actions not words, preserve the ideals of the Constitution and the Founding Fathers.

We have returned the republic to one focused on protecting us from our enemies and creating opportunities for all citizens of the United States instead of controlling and meddling in their lives. We have again realized how important our freedom is, the sacrifices which have been made for it, and vowed to never let a few people rule over us in our best interest because we know they will do no such thing. We have never come so close to returning to the old ways of the rest of the world left behind hundreds of years ago in search of new and better opportunities in the new world of America. We have walked down the easy path of government control and dependency and seen its price is too high. A price that sentences us and our children to a life where we can no longer say the sky is the limit and that one is only limited by one's self because those words would have no longer been true. We have chosen the path where those words again have real meaning and have chosen the difficult path to protect our part of the American dream and the American Way.

Lastly, I would want to refer again to my dedication made at the beginning of this book and say a few words to those in and outside of our government that would take away my freedom and liberty and that of every other U.S. Citizen:

Stand by… We The People are paying attention, we are watching, we are taking action, and we are not going away!

Let Freedom ring!
We *will* make it happen.

<u>The Pledge of Allegiance</u>

I pledge allegiance to the flag

of the United States of America,

and to the republic for which it stands,

one nation

under God,

indivisible,

with liberty and justice for all.

This U.S. Citizen

For author contact or comment please write to:

This U.S. Citizen
P.O. Box 3386
Cedar Park, Texas 78630-3386

www.ingramcontent.com/pod-product-compliance
Lightning Source LLC
Chambersburg PA
CBHW020414290526
45785CB00002B/560